Prizing His Passion

PRIZING HIS PASSION

*Why the Death of Jesus Christ Should Matter to You
. . . a Forty-Six-Day Journey*

JOHN S. OLDFIELD

RESOURCE *Publications* • Eugene, Oregon

PRIZING HIS PASSION
Why the Death of Jesus Christ Should Matter to You . . . a Forty-Six-Day Journey

Copyright © 2019 John S. Oldfield. All rights reserved. Except for brief quotations in critical publications or reviews, no part of this book may be reproduced in any manner without prior written permission from the publisher. Write: Permissions, Wipf and Stock Publishers, 199 W. 8th Ave., Suite 3, Eugene, OR 97401.

Resource Publications
An Imprint of Wipf and Stock Publishers
199 W. 8th Ave., Suite 3
Eugene, OR 97401

www.wipfandstock.com

PAPERBACK ISBN: 978-1-5326-7142-5
HARDCOVER ISBN: 978-1-5326-7143-2
EBOOK ISBN: 978-1-5326-7144-9

Manufactured in the U.S.A.   FEBRUARY 12, 2021

To my beloved wife,

DAGMAR OLDFIELD

... the most exemplary
wife, mother,
grandmother, and
co-laborer
a pastor
could ever have
for
his family and
ministry

... with my
heartfelt gratitude
for well over
half a century
of life and service
together

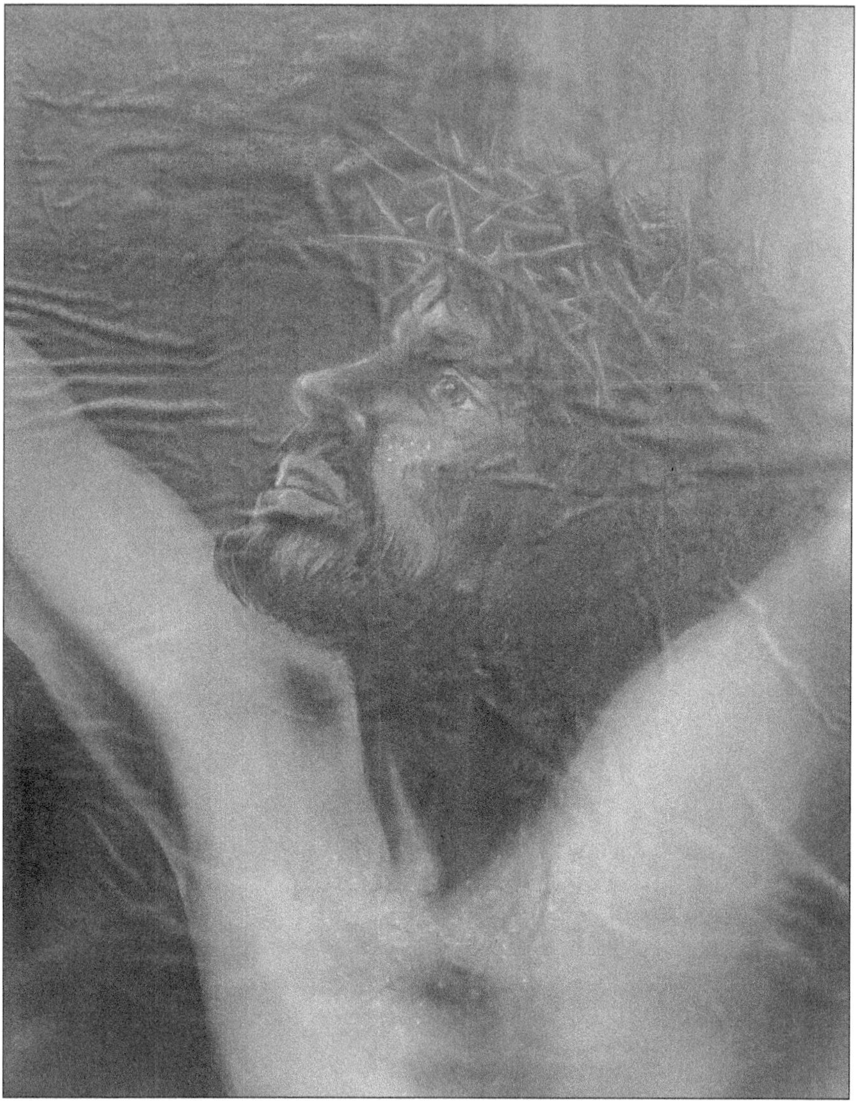

In Fond Memory of

Linda Colleen Leebrick

February 24, 1953—April 21, 1976

Linda was the artist who created the original 30 x 40-inch, chalk drawing of Jesus' crucifixion in color, seen to the left in black and white. She did it "from scratch" during a multi-media presentation at a county-wide Good Friday Service held in the tiny town of Levant, Kansas, in the early 1970s. Since Linda had no further plans for her magnifcent drawing, I asked if I could have it. Unknown to me, after putting some final touches on it, she took it to a glass company to have it framed and covered with non-glare glass.

Unfortunately, company personnel cut the newsprint paper, on which she had produced the drawing, from the large piece of cardboard or posterboard around which she had stretched it, thereby creating multiple wrinkles in the paper. Even after pressing it under glass for forty-eight hours, they could not eliminate the wrinkles. Although, sadly, they can be seen throughout the picture, they add an unusual "dimension" to it when it is viewed in person. Dr. Vernon Grounds—then president of my alma mater, now known as Denver Seminary—said it was the greatest depiction of The Passion he'd ever seen.

Linda was one of the finest and most talented, yet humblest and most spiritually dedicated young adults my wife and I have ever known. While she was a student at Colby Community College, she became involved with "The Alternative," the coffee-house ministry we operated in Colby, Kansas, from 1970 to 1974, and then in the Levant Community Church, the congregation we pastored from 1967 to 1974. Among other wonderful memories of her presence among us, I vividly recall her avid interest in the Bible studies I conducted for young adults in that old hotel-basement coffee house and her service as a counselor during teen-week at the camp our Fellowship then owned in the Rocky Mountains.

Raised by two wise, talented, and devoted Christian parents on a farm in Atwood, Kansas, Linda was dearly loved and immensely respected by all who knew her, including her art students at the high school in Hill City,

Kansas, where she taught upon her graduation from CCC and then Kansas State University (cum laude). Tragically, on the night of April 21, 1976, Linda was violently abducted from her apartment in Hill City and, during an apparent attempted rape, was brutally bludgeoned to death with tree branches by a crazed neighbor from across the street. She died defending her purity and in so many ways left a lasting legacy of spiritual commitment. Officers with the Kansas Bureau of Investigation said they had never investigated the murder of a person with such an impeccable reputation.

Thanks to her testimony for Christ, many were brought to faith in Him because of her death—through her funeral, through an article that appeared much later in a crime magazine, and through a variety of personal conversations with those who knew her. Her spiritual legacy lives on, now well into the twenty-first century—including through her artwork. She would want me to direct any praise to her crucified, risen Lord.

Contents

Permissions | xi

Preface | xiii

Day 1   Introduction | 1
Day 2   Pinch Hitter | 4
Day 3   Two Passover Anomalies | 9
Day 4   Surely Not I? | 13
Day 5   The Cross and the Problem of Suffering and Evil | 16
Day 6   Faith that Fits the Facts | 20
Day 7   Who Killed Jesus Christ? (Part 1) | 24
Day 8   Who Killed Jesus Christ? (Part 2) | 29
Day 9   What Jesus Experienced on the Cross (Part 1) | 32
Day 10 What Jesus Experienced on the Cross (Part 2) | 36
Day 11 What Jesus Experienced on the Cross (Part 3) | 39
Day 12 Why Celebrate the Lord's Supper? | 43
Day 13 What the Suffering Servant is Like | 48
Day 14 He Loves Us | 51
Day 15 A Poignant Story from Bedouin Culture | 55
Day 16 Blood in the River | 59
Day 17 The Price of the Harvest | 63
Day 18 How I Got In | 68
Day 19 Sharing in His Sufferings | 71
Day 20 Dying Daily | 75

Day 21	Forgiveness—Amish-Style	79
Day 22	Donating Blood to an Enemy	82
Day 23	The Unthinkable God	85
Day 24	The Pitfall of the Once-for-All Sacrifice	90
Day 25	Four Crosses	93
Day 26	Don't Forget Gethsemane—the Agony of Decision!	97
Day 27	Don't Forget Gabbatha—the Agony of Desecration!	101
Day 28	Don't Forget Golgotha—the Agony of Death!	106
Day 29	Don't Forget Galilee—the Agony of Declaration	109
Day 30	The Lifting Up of the Son of Man	114
Day 31	Whatever Became of Barabbas?	118
Day 32	Body Piercing Saved My Life!	124
Day 33	Immediate Access	127
Day 34	The Greatest Rescue	132
Day 35	No Place in Me	136
Day 36	The Stigmata	141
Day 37	Room at the Cross	145
Day 38	Clean!	148
Day 39	Purged!	152
Day 40	Reconciliation	158
Day 41	Pearl Harbor and the God of Reconciliation	163
Day 42	Monkey Business	167
Day 43	Money Business	171
Day 44	Theories of the Atonement (Part 1)	175
Day 45	Theories of the Atonement (Part 2)	180
Day 46	Conclusion	184
	Benediction	187

Bibliography | 189

Permissions

Scripture taken from the NEW AMERICAN STANDARD BIBLE®, Copyright © 1960, 1962, 1963, 1968, 1971, 1972, 1973, 1975, 1977, 1995 by The Lockman Foundation. Used by permission.

Permission for extensive quotation (Aileen Coleman's Bedouin story) from *The Name* by Franklin Graham on Day 15 granted by Erin Gonzales, Subsidiary Rights Manager for HarperCollins Christian Publishing, on October 16, 2018.

Permission for extensive quotation (Del Tarr's West Africa story) from *Leadership Journal* on Day 17 granted by Jacob Walsh, Vice President and Publisher for christianitytoday.com on October 15, 2018.

Permission for extensive quotation (John Piper's commentary on suffering) from *What Jesus Demands from the World* on Day 19 granted by Nicole Gosling, Licensing and Permissions Services Manager for Crossway on October 17, 2018.

Permission for extensive quotations from *Breakpoint* commentaries by Charles Colson on Days 21 and 22 granted by Sherrie Irvin of the Colson Center for Christian Worldview on October 23, 2018.

Permission for extensive quotation (John Fieldsend's commentary on the pitfall of the once-for-all sacrifice) from *Encounter with God* on Day 24 granted by Blaine Bergey, Business Manager for Scripture Union, on October 24, 2018.

Preface

Love was compressed for all history in that lonely, bleeding figure. Jesus, who had said He could call down angels at any moment and rescue Himself from the horror, chose not to—because of us. For God so loved us that He sent His only Son to die for us.

—Philip Yancey[1]

The word "passion" evokes various meanings. It can connote a strong and barely controllable emotion such as love or hate; a defense attorney might say, "It was a crime of passion." It can connote an instance or experience of strong romantic love or sexual desire; a romance writer might say, "They embraced each other in a flood of passion." It can connote a strong or extravagant fondness, enthusiasm, or desire for *anything*; we might say of a friend or relative, "His passion is classical music," or "Her passion is interior decorating."

But the word "Passion" with a capital "P," which appears in the title of this book and is central to its contents, refers uniquely to Jesus Christ.[2] Linguistically, in this context, the word derives from the perfect-tense participial form—*passus*—of the Latin verb *pati*, meaning "to suffer." It includes everything Jesus *suffered* from the time of His anguished prayer and arrest on Thursday night in the Garden of Gethsemane through His agonizing

---

1. Yancey, *Where Is God When It Hurts?* 162.

2. For example, *The St. Matthew Passion*, widely regarded as one of the masterpieces of classical sacred music, is an oratorio written by Johann Sebastian Bach in 1727 that sets chapters 26 and 27 of the Gospel of Matthew (in the German translation of Martin Luther) to music. Its original title, translated into English, is "The Passion of our Lord Jesus Christ according to the Evangelist Matthew." It's about His sufferings.

Preface

death on the cross on Friday afternoon (what we have come to call "Good Friday"). It's *that* Passion we will explore together in these pages.

I've prepared this volume of meditations on His sufferings to assist you in thinking about them in fresh ways. I've not intended that it be read straight through in one sitting. It's meant to be read devotionally, one chapter a day for forty-six days, especially during Lent—for those who observe that season of the year and for those who might like to start doing so.[3] It can also be read one chapter a week for forty-six weeks, especially on Sunday.

If you're not yet a follower of Jesus Christ but are curious about Him, I hope this book will help you understand His mission on earth, give you a glimpse of His immense love for you, and even lead you into a transformative relationship with Him. In whatever manner you choose to use this book, I trust it will be of real benefit to you.

John S. Oldfield

---

3. If you include the six Sundays (which, if fasting is involved on all the other days of the week, are often *excluded*), Lent lasts for forty-six days (instead of forty). It begins on Ash Wednesday and ends on the day between Good Friday and Easter Sunday.

Day 1

Introduction

*Though the cross repels, it also attracts.
It possesses a magnetic quality.*

Billy Graham[1]

Uncontrollable sobbing, anguished weeping, wrenching grief, shocked disappointment, and overwhelming despair! These are often the reactions of tribal people witnessing the horrific abuse inflicted upon Jesus of Nazareth as they view the film *Jesus* in their native language and learn of Him for the first time. They rejoice over His kindness to marginalized people, His miraculous healings of sick or handicapped people, and His revolutionary teachings. But then—in an awful turn of events—they see Him cleverly betrayed, roughly arrested, cruelly mocked, unjustly tried, brutally beaten, horribly tortured, agonizingly crucified, and heartbreakingly entombed. They are so consumed with sorrow that they can hardly stand it until, as the real-life drama continues to unfold on the screen, they realize that He has come back from the dead and is alive again! They can barely contain their relief and ecstasy!

1. Graham, *The Reason for My Hope*, page unknown by me. Billy Graham, the evangelist who proclaimed the Passion and the resurrection of Jesus Christ to more people than anyone in history (live audiences of nearly 215 million), died—thereby transitioning to the heaven about which he also so often preached—on February 21, 2018, at the age of ninety-nine.

The truth of the gospel of Jesus Christ is not old-hat to them; it's totally fresh, it's deeply moving, and it's life-changing! Reputable written and video reports from Jesus Film Project personnel challenge the apathy that often sets in among those of us who have been exposed to the gospel for years, even decades. We've learned that, after some showings of the film, even terrorists have come to transforming faith in Jesus!

Saul of Tarsus was once a terrorist of sorts "breathing threats and murder against the disciples of the Lord" (Acts 9:1).[2] Mercifully, through a supernatural vision, he was dramatically converted to faith in the crucified, resurrected Messiah (Acts 9:3–19); even his name was eventually changed, and he became the now-legendary apostle Paul (which, appropriately, means "little," "small," or "humble").[3] Unable to forget the horrifically misguided, zealous activity of his pre-conversion days, he forever viewed himself as the number-one sinner in the history of humanity. He called himself "the very least of all saints [true believers]" (Eph 3:8, brackets mine) and wrote, "It is a trustworthy statement, deserving full acceptance, that Christ Jesus came into the world to save sinners, among whom I am foremost of all" (1 Tim 1:15).

For this reason, perpetually prizing the Passion of his Lord, he reminded the believers at Corinth, Greece: "And when I came to you, brethren, I did not come with superiority of speech or of wisdom, proclaiming to you the testimony of God. For I determined to know nothing among you except Jesus Christ, and Him crucified" (1 Cor 2:1–2). To the believers in Galatia he wrote, "But may it never be that I would boast, except in the cross of our Lord Jesus Christ, through which the world has been crucified to me, and I to the world" (Gal 6:14).

The cross was inestimably important to Paul and can be for *us*—regardless of the particular pit from which *we* were rescued. That's why Jesus instituted what we call "The Lord's Supper" on the eve of His crucifixion. As He held up the common unleavened bread and the ordinary table wine of the ancient Passover meal and imbued them with a new significance, He told His disciples, "Do this in remembrance of Me" (Luke 22:19). Paul later explained, "For as often as you eat this bread and drink the cup, you

---

2. All Scriptural quotations, unless otherwise noted, will be from the *New American Standard Bible*, specifically from the (updated) *NASB Study Bible*.

3. An outstanding motion picture, "Paul, Apostle of Christ," was released in theaters across the United States on March 23, 2018, with James Faulkner as Paul and Jim Caviezel as Luke. It is set in Paul's last days, when he was under detention in Rome prior to his execution. It is now available on DVD.

1—Introduction

proclaim the Lord's death until He comes" (1 Cor 11:6). Thus, Steve Brown of the Key Life Network has wryly observed, "The world drinks to forget; the Christian drinks to remember."[4]

Sometimes believers think that reflecting regularly on the Passion of the Lord is elementary, even boring, and a sign of immaturity, not spiritual depth. Nothing could be further from the truth! The fact is: anyone who thinks he has somehow in his Christian walk gone "beyond the cross" has actually backslidden! He has failed to see the centrality of the cross in the incarnation and mission of Jesus on earth. He has failed to see the centrality of the cross in the justification, sanctification, and glorification of the believer.[5] He has failed to understand that the scars from the wounds Jesus sustained will be visible on His body—the body in which He appeared after His resurrection—for all eternity! He has failed to grasp the fact that we'll never stop praising Jesus for what He accomplished on that hill outside the city of Jerusalem.

I share the passion of Scottish pastor George F. MacLeod *about* the Passion:

> The cross must be raised again at the center of the marketplace as well as on the steeple of the church. I am claiming that Jesus was not crucified in a cathedral between two candles, but on a cross between two thieves; at a crossroads so cosmopolitan they had to write His title in Hebrew, Latin, and Greek; at the kind of place where cynics talk smut, and thieves curse, and soldiers gamble; because that is where He died and that is what He died about, and that is where churchmen ought to be and what churchmen should be about.[6]

---

4. Brown, quoted by Colson, *The Body*, 127.

5. Don't be turned off by these four theological terms! *Incarnation* is what happened when the Creator-God of the universe slipped into the life-stream of humanity through the conception and birth of Jesus of Nazareth in and from the womb of a young Jewish virgin named Mary. *Justification* is what happens when you repent of your sin, place your trust in Jesus Christ and what He accomplished for you on the cross, and receive forgiveness and right-standing before the holy God of the universe. *Sanctification* is being set apart for God's purposes; it's what begins to happen at the moment you're justified, continues happening as you grow in your relationship with God, and ultimately and completely happens at your death and transition to heaven. *Glorification* is what happens when you arrive in heaven, begin eternity with Christ, and experience total freedom from sin.

6. MacLeod, *Only One Way Left*, 38.

Day 2

PINCH HITTER

*He came to pay a debt He didn't owe,
because we owed a debt we couldn't pay.*

—AUTHOR UNKNOWN

I NOW LIVE IN Peoria, Arizona, which boasts one of the spring-training stadiums for Major League Baseball. Florida hosts the *Citrus* League games, while Arizona hosts the *Cactus* League contests. The team with the biggest draw in the Cactus League each year is the Chicago Cubs. Given their record over the last century of seasons, this is an amazing phenomenon. Although the Cubs are one of the only two remaining charter members of the National League, they had not won a World Series championship since 1908—a longer dry spell than that of any other major North American professional sports team of any genre . . . until November 2, 2016! The hapless but ever hopeful Cubs hadn't even won a League pennant since 1945 (the year I became a Cubs fan at the age of five), and they lost the World Series that year to the Detroit Tigers. To be a Cubs fan year after year has required the utmost in wishful optimism or dogged fidelity—or both.

But in the 2016 season, the Cubs had the best win-loss percentage in the Major Leagues, and they went on to win *both* the National League pennant *and* the World Series, and they did the latter in a seventh game that couldn't have been more dramatic if it had been a Hollywood movie! They

2—Pinch Hitter

beat a totally worthy American League opponent, the fiercely competitive Cleveland Indians . . . in Cleveland . . . after a short rain delay . . . in the tenth inning . . . by one run . . . eight to seven . . . in one of the best professional baseball games ever played! As a Cubs fan who, I admit, had almost given up on them, I was so excited I could hardly stand it! That leads me to relate to you one of my greatest *vicarious* thrills in sports.

It came during the second game of a double-header the Cubs were playing at Wrigley Field with the Philadelphia Phillies on July 29, 1951. The Cubs were up to bat in the last half of the seventh inning. The Phillies were ahead four to two, there were two outs, and the bases were loaded. The pitcher, Dutch Leonard, was scheduled to bat, but suddenly the announcer blared over the public-address system that there was to be a pinch-hitter. Phil Cavarretta had become the playing-manager of the Chicago Cubs just eight days earlier, and he had decided to put *himself* in the lineup at that moment as a pinch hitter. Think of the tension, think of the excitement, and think of the pressure! How would *you* like to have been in his cleats just then?

For all practical purposes, the game was at stake! He was the Cubs' only hope! Can you imagine what happened? Phil Cavarretta stepped to the plate and, wasting no time, drove the great Robin Roberts's first pitch—an inside slider—into the right field bleachers for a grand-slam home run, Cavarretta's first-ever!! The Cubs went on to win the game by two runs, eight to six! It was Cavarretta's biggest thrill as a player and mine as a fan![1]

The dictionary defines a pinch hitter as "a substitute who, usually at some critical moment of the game, bats for another." Many preachers have compared the game of baseball to the game of life, and I'd like to join them by suggesting to you that Jesus Christ was the greatest pinch hitter of all time. I say that for two reasons: because He pinch-hit at a critical moment in the game, and because He hit the greatest home run ever hit.

First of all, then, He pinch-hit at a critical moment in the game. When we had discovered we had no strength even to get up to the plate to bat, He

---

1. I have reconstructed the details of this game with the help of baseball websites on the internet. In my obviously fallible—though youthfully enthusiastic—memory, however, the details were even more dramatic! (I had just turned eleven years old twenty-two days before this game.) It was the bottom half of the *ninth* inning, not the *seventh*; the four-bagger came *after a full-count*, not on the *first* pitch; the Cubs were down by *three* runs, not *two*; and they went on to finish *fifth* in the league, not *eighth* (last). *That* record occurred not in *1951* but in *1952*. I like my story better! Alas, in the interest of accuracy, I have changed it to reflect what, apparently, are the *actual* details.

stepped in and voluntarily offered to take our place in the batter's box. You see, St. Paul says, "While we were still helpless, at the right time Christ" stepped up, not to the batter's box but to the cross, the place of execution, and "died for the ungodly" (Rom 5:6). We had no strength; we were sinners by birth and by choice; we were helplessly guilty before God and hopelessly lost for eternity. We were wandering about on a broad road that led down a slippery slope into ultimate destruction when Jesus intervened. We were without hope and without God in this world (Eph 2:12). "But God demonstrate[d] His own love toward us, in that while we were yet sinners, Christ died for us" (Rom 5:8, brackets mine).

We'd tried everything we could to fix our desperate situation—to no avail. But then Jesus intervened. He said, "Stop trying. I'll go to bat for you." He was *God's* "pinch hitter," for, as St. Peter put it, He was "delivered up by the predetermined plan and foreknowledge of God" (Acts 2:23). So, He stepped up to the plate, eyed the best pitch of the opposing team's pitcher, and took a cut at it. His timing was perfect. It was a curveball, but He connected with it, belted it out of the park, rounded the bases, touched home, came back into the dugout, and corrected the score-sheet to make it look as though *we*—who were nothing but strikeout kings—had done it ourselves!

Paul says that God made Jesus, who had never sinned, "who knew no sin, to *be* sin on our behalf, that we might become the righteousness of God in Him" (2 Cor 5:21, italics mine). God made Jesus, who had never struck out, who, in fact, had a batting average of 1.000, take our place, feel for a few horrible hours like the worst hitter and fielder in history, and then hit a home run for us, making it look as though we, who would one day trust Him, had hit that four-bagger and had played errorless ball in the field! There's no doubt about it: God's "pinch hitter," Jesus Christ, pinch-hit at a critical, crucial moment of the game!

But I'm also saying that Jesus Christ was the greatest pinch hitter of all time because He hit the greatest home run ever hit. He made it possible for us to have a home in heaven. Millions will make the trip around the bases to home plate—to heaven—because of Him. He took our place on the cross, suffered hell for us there, died in our place, rose from the dead, returned to the right hand of God the Father in heaven, and thereby opened the door to heaven for us. Even as He hung on that cross, He made a promise to a criminal dying on the cross next to His: "Today you shall be with Me in paradise" (Luke 23:43).

2 — Pinch Hitter

Ever since Jesus' death and resurrection, for the born-again, blood-bought believer, to die is to be "absent from the body" and to be "at home with the Lord"—present with Him (2 Cor 5:8). You see, "to live is Christ, to die is gain" (Phil 1:21). Not only will we believers one day be *with* Him; we'll also be "*like* Him, because we will see Him just as He is" (1 John 3:2, italics mine). It's inspiring to reflect on the fact that departed loved ones who have put their trust in Him and sought to live for Him here on earth are, from the moment of their death, with Him in person, having gained the fullness of eternal life. They're home! And they've been totally sanctified—glorified, if you please; they're *with* Jesus and they're *like* Him! If you're a true believer, it will be that way for you, too. Truly, Jesus Christ hit the greatest home run ever hit. It took His sinless life, His sacrificial death, and His supernatural resurrection to accomplish it, but He did it!

By the way, if you believe you're in a permanent batting slump and that you desperately need a pinch hitter, if you believe that Jesus Christ is God's substitute for *you*, if you believe that He rose from the dead for *you*, if you tell Him you can't make it without Him, and if you embrace Him as your sin-bearer, you can win the "*spiritual* World Series" battle for your soul.

Not only that, but, since everybody loves an underdog, angels in the bleachers of heaven will stand to their feet and applaud and cheer; for Jesus said, "There is joy in the presence of the angels of God over one sinner who repents" (Luke 15:10). I don't know how many angels there are in heaven, but there were at least 72,000 ready to defend Jesus at the time of His arrest in the Garden of Gethsemane.[2] Thus, tens of thousands—maybe millions—of angels cheer when one sinner repents!

The official celebration in Chicago for the Cubs' victory on November 4, 2016, drew an estimated *five million* people and became the seventh largest human (not angelic!) gathering in world history and the largest in the history of the United States of America![3] But as big as it was, that celebra-

---

2. Jesus said that His Father could put "more than twelve legions of angels" at His disposal (Matt 26:53). At that time, Rome, through its army, ruled the then-known world (including Israel), and a Roman legion consisted of about 6,000 soldiers. Thus, Jesus could have requested more than 72,000 angels to come to His defense. Of course, for all we know, there may well be *millions* of angels.

3. Interestingly, on October 15, during the first game of the 2016 National League Championship Series, in which the Cubs were playing the Los Angeles Dodgers, the teams were tied 3–3 in the bottom of the eighth inning. Cubs Manager Joe Maddon sent former Arizona Diamondbacks catcher Miguel Montero to the plate as a pinch hitter. The bases were loaded. Montero hit one of the only three pinch-hit, grand slam home

tion will be dwarfed by the one when Jesus Christ returns to earth with all His angels and with the saints of all the ages (Matt 24:30–31; 25:31)! Then His angels (no, not the Los Angeles Angels of Anaheim!) will *really* rejoice!

---

runs ever hit in Major League Baseball post-season history! The score was then 7–3, augmented to 8–3 when the next batter, Dexter Fowler, followed the grand slam with a solo four-bagger of his own! Keep in mind, though, that while Miguel Montero's manager inserted him into the lineup, Phil Cavarretta, who *was* the manager, inserted *himself* into the lineup back in 1951! And *that* makes a better illustration of what Jesus did for us!

Day 3

Two Passover Anomalies

> *In a world where success is the measure and justification of all things the figure of Him who was sentenced and crucified remains a stranger and is at best the object of pity . . . The figure of the Crucified invalidates all thought which takes success for its standard.*
>
> —Dietrich Bonhoeffer[1]

Among the other anomalies associated with His final Passover, the last meal Jesus of Nazareth would share with His closest disciples on the eve of His crucifixion, two stand out. They both show up in chapter 13 of John's Gospel. On the surface, neither makes a bit of sense. Both pertain to the identity and activity of the primary figure in this whole amazing scenario. What are they?

The first one shows us the astonishing *humility* of that primary figure. Who was he? Well, he was Jesus, the second person of the triune Godhead, God wrapped in human skin. Look at the record: "Jesus, knowing that the Father had given all things into His hands, and that He had come forth from God and was going back to God, got up from supper, and laid aside

---

1. Bonhoeffer, "Rethinking Our Ideas about Success," *Dietrich Bonhoeffer: Writings Selected with an Introduction by Robert Coles*, page unknown by me.

His garments; and taking a towel, He girded Himself. Then He poured water into the basin and began to wash the disciples' feet and to wipe them with the towel with which He was girded" (John 13:3–5).

Wait a minute! The Apostle John, who was present on this occasion, records that Jesus was in full awareness of His own identity and dignity. He knew that God the Father had given all things into His hands. He knew that He had come to this earth from God in heaven. And He knew that He was going back to God in heaven. Yet the next thing John says is that the God-man laid aside His outer garments, girded Himself with a towel, poured water in a basin, and—taking the role of a household slave—began washing His disciples' dusty feet and wiping them with the towel!

What's wrong with this picture? First of all, from the standpoint of common sense and theological propriety, God should never have become a human being to begin with. (Just ask any devout Jew or Muslim.) But now that He had, surely He should have been waited upon, served, and catered to—not the reverse! Yet here He was, doing what a servant should have done or, absent such a person on this occasion, what one or more of His disciples should have done: provide the customary hospitality for guests in those days in that part of the world by washing their dirty feet.

No wonder the Apostle Paul would write years later, "Have this attitude in yourselves which was also in Christ Jesus, who, although He existed in the form of God, did not regard equality with God a thing to be grasped, but emptied Himself, taking the form of a bond-servant, and being made in the likeness of men" (Phil 2:5–7)! This was the Creator washing the dirty feet of His creatures! What astonishing, yet exemplary, humility!

The other of the two Passover anomalies shows us the astonishing *glory* of the primary figure in this whole scenario. It shows us the outrageous concept Jesus had of what it meant to "be glorified" and to "glorify" His Father. Look at the record: "Therefore when he [Judas, who was about to betray Jesus into the hands of His enemies] had gone out, Jesus said, 'Now is the Son of Man glorified, and God is glorified in Him; if God is glorified in Him, God will also glorify Him in Himself, and will glorify Him immediately'" (John 13:31–32, brackets mine).

To what was Jesus referring in this cryptic statement? Was it to the brilliance and splendor of His experience on the Mount of Transfiguration? No, that had already taken place. Was it to the kind of defeat of the Roman Empire to which His disciples thought He was here on earth to accomplish? No, that was an erroneous assumption on their part. Was it to His return to

3 — Two Passover Anomalies

the Father—His yet-future ascension? No, although that was part of it. Was it to His spectacular return one day to the same place from which He would depart from this planet? No, that was a long way off; in fact, it's now nearly two thousand years since He uttered the enigmatic words.

To what then, was He referring? To His impending suffering and death! In other words, He was looking ahead to the rest of that night, the next morning, and the next afternoon—during which He was going to be arrested, "cuffed," tried (in a giant miscarriage of justice), mocked, spat upon, whipped, punched, struck, cut, bruised, nailed to two crossbeams, and killed. And He was indicating that all of this would result in His glorification and the glorification of His Father! Equally shocking, Isaiah had prophesied that "the Lord [would be] *pleased* to crush Him, putting Him to grief" (Isa 53:10a, brackets and italics mine). And Paul would later say to the believers in Ephesus that "Christ also loved you, and gave Himself up for us, an offering and a sacrifice to God as *a fragrant aroma*" (Eph 5:2, italics mine).

What?? How could that be?? How could such violence and injustice possibly glorify God the Son and God the Father? I suggest the following answers:

- Because of the way Jesus handled it.
- Because of the absence of any retaliation on His part.
- Because of His willingness to go through it, to endure it.
- Because, in submission to His Father, He was fulfilling His Father's will, the divine plan. In fact, that's exactly what He said later that same night in His great high-priestly prayer: "I glorified You on the earth, having accomplished the work which You have given Me to do. Now, Father, glorify Me together with Yourself, with the glory which I had with You before the world was" (John 17:4–5).
- Because He was offering Himself up as an atonement for the sins of the human race, including the very people clamoring for, engineering, and carrying out His execution.
- Because "as a result of the anguish of His soul, He [would] see it [the goal of bridging the gap between God and man, the just dying for the unjust] and be satisfied; by His knowledge the Righteous One [would] justify the many, as He [would] bear their iniquities" (Isa 53:11, brackets mine).

- Because "for the *joy* set before Him [Jesus] endured the cross, despising the shame, and has sat down at the right hand of the throne of God" (Heb 12:2, italics and brackets mine). What was "the joy" to which He was looking forward? *We* were—we redeemed human beings, we sinners saved by His amazing grace!

No unredeemed human being would ever think of the grisly, ghastly torture and death of Jesus of Nazareth as a way for Him to be glorified or the blood and shame of the cross as a way for His Father to be glorified! What an astounding concept of glorification! No wonder Paul would later admit that "the word of the cross is foolishness to those who are perishing," and then add, "but to us who are being saved it is the power of God" (1 Cor 1:18)! No wonder, as mentioned in the introduction to this volume, he would later write, "May it never be that I would boast [or glory], except in the cross of our Lord Jesus Christ, through which the world has been crucified to me, and I to the world" (Gal 6:14, brackets mine)![2]

Two Passover anomalies: Jesus' startling *humility* and His shocking concept of *glory*. By God's grace, we too need to demonstrate that kind of humility; and, in the light of what was accomplished there, we too need to glory or boast only in the cross!

---

2. According to Don Wilton, Billy Graham's pastor for the last fifteen years of his life, this is the verse the world-renowned evangelist would like to have preached from if he'd been physically able to conduct one last crusade. It's also the verse he handpicked for Pastor Wilton to preach from at his burial, which, as it turned out, took place on March 2, 2018. Shellnutt, "What It Was Like to Be Billy Graham's Pastor," *Christianity Today*.

Day 4

SURELY NOT I?

The depravity of man is at once the most empirically verifiable reality but at the same time the most intellectually resisted fact.

—MALCOLM MUGGERIDGE[1]

THE PROPHET JEREMIAH SAID, "The heart is more deceitful than all else and is desperately sick; who can understand it?" (Jer 17:9) And the apostle Paul said, "I know that nothing good dwells in me, that is, in my flesh; for the willing is present in me, but the doing of the good is not" (Rom 7:18). That's why we're all "prone to wander," as the songwriter Robert Robinson put it in his great hymn, "Come, Thou Fount of Every Blessing."[2] That's why British-born Alan Redpath, while he was the highly esteemed pastor of historic Moody Church in downtown Chicago, could say—as he did when I heard him preach in an Ohio town, "Ladies and gentlemen, but for the grace of God, I am perfectly capable of walking out of this building after this service tonight and committing the worst sin imaginable."

That's why, at the last supper and last Passover Jesus would celebrate with His twelve disciples during His first visit to this planet, He could predict the impending failures of *all* of them to stand with Him in His hour of

---

1. Muggeridge, quoted in Zacharias, *Cries of the Heart*, page unknown by me.
2. Robinson, "Come, Thou Fount of Every Blessing," 1757 (public domain).

greatest need. I invite you to examine with me one of the accounts of the dialogue at the table in that upper room—the account in Mark 14:

> When it was evening, He came with the twelve. As they were reclining at table and eating, Jesus said, "Truly I say to you that *one* of you will betray Me—the one who is eating with Me." They began to be grieved and to say to Him one by one, "Surely not I?" And He said to them, "It is one of the twelve, one who dips with Me in the bowl . . ." (vv. 17–20, italics mine) . . .
>
> And Jesus said to them, "You will *all* fall away, because it is written, 'I will strike down the shepherd, and the sheep shall be scattered.'" . . . But Peter said to Him, "Even though all may fall away, yet *I* will not." And Jesus said to him, "Truly I say to you, that this very night, before a rooster crows twice, you yourself will deny Me three times." But Peter kept saying insistently, "Even if I have to die with You, I will not deny You!" And they *all* were saying the same thing also (vv. 29–31, italics mine).

In spite of Judas's knowledge of his plan to betray Jesus into the hands of His enemies that very night and the stout insistence of Peter and all the others that they would *not* deny Him, even upon threat of death, when Jesus first unveiled the stark reality that one of them was going to betray Him, they *all* "began to be grieved and to say to Him one by one, 'Surely not I?'"

Yes, perhaps they meant: "Not *I*! You can count on *me*, Lord! *I* would *never* do such a thing!" But the fact that the response of each took the form of a question suggests that each caught a brief, worried glimpse of the weakness, the depravity, the unpredictability, and the potential for unspeakable failure and evil that lay within his own soul. Each asked Jesus, hesitantly, "Surely not *I*? You're not talking about *me* . . . *are* You?? I would *never* do such a despicable deed . . . would I? I *couldn't* . . . *could* I?"

If you're a Christ-follower and a church member, visualize yourself seated at the meeting place for your congregation's next observance of The Lord's Supper. What if Jesus were sitting at the Communion Table and predicted that someone there in the room was about to betray Him or deny Him or fall away from a previous stand for Him? What would *you* say? Would you say, "That's terrible, Lord! Who's the traitor who would do that? *I* certainly wouldn't . . . *would* I? Surely it's not *I* of whom you speak . . . *is* it? Surely not *I*?" I believe *all* of your fellow-congregants would squirm uncomfortably (as would I, if I were there), glance nervously at one another,

4—Surely Not I?

and, as Luke tells us the original twelve disciples did (Luke 22:23), begin to discuss among ourselves which one of us was going to do this thing.

As we all know, Judas did betray Jesus that night into the hands of His enemies, Peter did three times deny even knowing Him, and all twelve did forsake Him and flee when He was arrested (Mark 14:50). What about us? What about you? Have you ever really failed the Lord, ever really collapsed in the clutch, ever wimped out when the going got tough? *Have* you? If not, then thank God for His grace and strength; but pay close attention to Paul's words: "Let him who thinks he stands take heed that he does not fall" (1 Cor 10:12).

But if you *have* ever really failed the Lord, how did you feel? If you've done so recently, the better question is, "How *do* you feel?" Did you—or do you—feel a horrible sense of guilt? Did you—or do you—feel an agonizing sense of grief? If so, have you come—or will you come now—to Jesus to bare your soul, pour it all out before Him, and let Him forgive and cleanse and heal you and bind up your broken heart?

Have you found that the Lord is near to him who has a broken heart (Ps 34:18)? Have you learned with David of old that "The steps of a man are established by the Lord; and He delights in his way," that "when he falls, he shall not be hurled headlong; because the Lord is the One who holds his hand" (Ps 37:23-24)? Have you learned with the apostle John that "if we confess our sins, He is faithful and righteous to forgive us our sins and to cleanse us from all unrighteousness" (1 John 1:9)?

Tragically, Judas didn't stick around long enough to be forgiven and restored; he took his own life. But Peter *did*, and he *was*. Have you learned with Peter that your faith *hasn't* failed and that, once you're straightened out and resting in Jesus' strength and not your own, He will actually use you to strengthen others (Luke 22:31-32)? During a post-resurrection breakfast on the shore of the Sea of Galilee, Jesus asked Peter three times, "Do you love Me?" In near exasperation, Peter thrice assured his Lord that he did. Indicating that He believed him, Jesus assigned him the monumental task of caring for new believers—lambs—and believers in general—sheep (John 21:15-17). Putting a whole different spin on the question the disciples asked Jesus on the eve of His crucifixion, Peter might well have been thinking there on the beach, "Surely not *I*?"

Day 5

THE CROSS AND THE PROBLEM OF SUFFERING AND EVIL

At the Cross, we see the absolute uniqueness
of the Christian response to suffering.
In Islam, the idea of God suffering is nonsense—
it is thought to make God weak.
In Buddhism, to reach divinity is precisely
to move beyond the possibility of suffering.
Only in Christ do we have a God
who is loving enough to suffer with us.

—*VINCE VITALE*[1]

IT WAS THURSDAY, NOVEMBER 15, 2001—just two months and four days after Islamic Jihadists deliberately crashed two airliners into the twin towers of the World Trade Center in lower Manhattan, taking the lives of 156 persons on board and over 2,600 on the ground . . . and just three days after human error caused American Airlines Flight 587 to crash into the Belle Harbor neighborhood of Queens, taking the lives of all 260 persons on board and another five on the ground. The former incident was the

---

1. Vitale, "If God, Why Suffering?" Ravi Zacharias International Ministries, August 28, 2014.

5—THE CROSS AND THE PROBLEM OF SUFFERING AND EVIL

deadliest single-day assault on civilians in U.S. history, and the latter was the second deadliest aviation accident to occur on U.S. soil.

Just before Pastor Darnell Bowman and I had left York, Pennsylvania, on the previous Monday in our York City Police Chaplains' van to head for New York City to offer whatever spiritual help we could to the personnel of the New York Police Department and the Port Authority Police Department, we learned of the crash in Queens. The detective who was our contact from the Midtown South Precinct in Manhattan indicated, once we got there, that we might be needed at the crash site that night, but as it turned out, no call came for our assistance. Thus, after spending Tuesday and Wednesday at Ground Zero, we found our way on Thursday to that horrible scene ourselves.

After a cordial visit with the priest at the Roman Catholic Church nearest the crash site, we went to the southwest corner of the taped-off area, where we watched lines of evidence specialists from the FBI and firefighters from the FDNY passing pieces of Airbus A300 wreckage and human body parts from one to another and then into designated containers for further examination. While we were standing there observing the somber scene, we struck up a conversation with a mail carrier for the United States Postal Service that was working his route on that beautiful November day. We learned that he had delivered mail in the community for many years, was acquainted with the people who had lost their lives on the ground three days earlier, and was acquainted with many of the fallen firefighters who had been residents of the same neighborhood—heroes who had lost their lives while trying to rescue civilians in the Twin Towers on September 11.

After we chatted briefly, he said, "Well, guys, I've got to get back to work." After watching him head down the block, we decided that we'd walk around to the east end of the crash site and see if we could get a better look at the grim proceedings and perhaps be of some help. Indeed, after running into two police chaplains from New Jersey whom I had met at regional seminars of the International Conference of Police Chaplains, we were asked to join them in praying over bags of body parts before they were transported by ambulance to the morgue at Bellevue Hospital in Manhattan. And later we chatted with and prayed for an exhausted Red Cross worker that had previously served in the more immediate aftermath of the September atrocity.

But as we were standing near the east entrance to the crash site, the postal service employee appeared again, still delivering mail on his familiar route. This time *he* approached us, and, looking directly at me, he said, "Chaplain, do you have a minute?" "Of course," I replied. Referring—without even saying so—to the horrific events of September 11 and November 12, he confessed, "I find myself getting very angry. How do *you* deal with all of this?" His comment implied a guarded complaint against the God who would allow such raw evil to manifest itself and such unthinkable devastation to occur. He was subtly raising the age-old dilemma of trying to reconcile God's alleged love and omnipotence with His seeming tolerance of evil and suffering. Although I don't recall my exact words, I know I said something pretty much like this in answer to the question raised by this sincere and caring man:

"I remember that this is not how it was at the beginning. When God created Adam and Eve, he placed them in an environment of beauty, order, and perfection—a place with no sin, no sickness, no violence, no accidents, no conflict, and no tragedies. It was the devil who tempted the first humans to disobey God, and it was they—exercising the free will He had given them—who flunked His simple test and plunged the entire race into sin, suffering, and death."

"And," I continued, "I realize that at the other end of human history, it won't be this way either. When God ushers in the new heavens and new earth, He is going to put everything right. There won't be any more crying or pain or death or mourning, and He's going to wipe away all tears from our eyes. It's once again going to be the way He intended the human experience to be."

"In the meantime," I explained, "He didn't just leave us to fend for ourselves. He sent His own Son from the splendor of heaven to the squalor of this messed-up planet to live among us, to show us His love, to teach us, to perform countless miracles, and, ultimately, to absorb all of our sin and evil in His own body as He died on that cruel Roman cross."

Before I could add much else, our new friend extended his right hand, shook mine, looked me in the eye with a smile on his face, and said, "I've got to go. But thanks, Chaplain! You've given me a whole new perspective on these matters!"

That perspective is called a biblical worldview. I've often wondered how people—especially first responders—can continue to function in the face of the tragic scenes they encounter day after day *without* the benefit of that worldview. No wonder so many use alcohol and drugs to escape the

5—The Cross and the Problem of Suffering and Evil

horror. No wonder so many contemplate taking their own lives, attempt to take them, and sometimes succeed.

I understand that a three-minute conversation at a horrific crash site does not solve the millennia-old dilemma about suffering and evil in human experience! Many have written brilliantly, thoroughly, lengthily, and sensitively on that subject. Their biblically-based reasoning is well worth reading. Let me simply say this as a conclusion to today's subject matter:

You and I need to *thank God* that, while we were yet sinners, Christ died for us on that dark Good Friday afternoon! We need to *thank God* that He burst forth from the tomb on that first Easter Sunday morning—conquering death and offering hope for this life and the next! The best thing we can do about suffering and evil in human experience is to open our hearts to Him, beseech Him to forgive *our* sins, and set out to follow Him in loving and merciful interaction with fellow-pilgrims and fellow-sufferers on our planet. Let's become part of the answer instead of part of the problem!

Day 6

FAITH THAT FITS THE FACTS

The Gospel of Christ and him crucified is still foolishness to millions who are perishing all over the world today.
How few people recognize that the answer to all the world's problems can be found at the foot of the cross.

—BILLY GRAHAM[1]

I HOPE YOU'RE AWARE of the fact that the gospel of Jesus Christ—which includes His death, His burial, His resurrection, and the implications thereof (1 Cor 15:1–5)—is true. It's good news, but it's also true news. That means that what we Christ-followers do every time we observe The Lord's Supper is rooted in actual history and accurate theology. In other words, unlike adherents of so many other religions and religious cults, we espouse a faith that fits the facts.

Our faith, "the faith which," according to Jude 3, "was once for all handed down to the saints," is historically and empirically true. Allow the aged apostle John to explain.

> What was from the beginning, what we have heard, what we have *seen* with our eyes, what we have *looked at* and *touched* with our hands, concerning the Word of Life—and the life was manifested, and we have *seen* and testify and proclaim to you the eternal life,

---

1. Graham, "The Power of the Cross," *Decision Magazine*, April 2007.

6 — Faith that Fits the Facts

> which was with the Father and was manifested to us—what we have *seen* and *heard* we proclaim to you also, so that you too may have fellowship with us; and indeed our fellowship is with the Father, and with His Son Jesus Christ. These things we write, so that our joy may be made complete (1 John 1:1-4, italics mine).

It's not: "Old Mother Hubbard went to the cupboard to give the poor dog a bone; when she came there, the cupboard was bare, and so the poor dog had none." It's: John and the other disciples *saw* Jesus turn the water into wine at a wedding reception in Cana of Galilee (John 2:1-11). Real people *saw* a real miracle at a real event in a real place.

It's not: "Poor Cinderella—she sat down and cried and cried and cried." It's: John and the other disciples *heard* Jesus pronounce words in Cana that healed a nobleman's son in Capernaum by the Sea of Galilee (John 4:46-54). Real people *heard* the real Messiah assure a real royal official that His real and terminally ill child in a real place was alive and well. And he was.

It's not: "Jack and Jill went up the hill to fetch a pail of water. Jack fell down and broke his crown, and Jill came tumbling after." It's: John and the other disciples *saw* Jesus heal a crippled man by the pool of Bethesda in Jerusalem (John 5:1-9). Real people *witnessed* the real, miraculous healing of a real person at a real place.

It's not: the three bears wondered who'd been eating their porridge and found out it was Goldilocks. It's: John and the other disciples *saw* Jesus feed 5,000 men—plus women and children—from the lunch of one small boy near the Sea of Galilee (John 6:1-14). They actually *touched* Jesus and, for that matter, the loaves and fish that multiplied exponentially before their very eyes as they handed them out to the crowd and as they collected the baskets full of leftovers. Real people participated in a real miracle of provision by a real Savior for real people with real hunger.

You get the point. These are actual events experienced by real people. Jesus' disciples *saw* Him walk on the water of the Sea of Galilee without sinking (John 6:15-21). They *saw* Him restore the sight of a blind man (John 9:1-7). They *saw* Him raise Lazarus from the dead (John 11:1-46). They *saw* Him, *heard* His voice, and *touched* Him after He died, was buried, and then emerged victorious over the grave (John 20:19-29). In fact, well over 500 people *saw* Him alive from the dead—500 at one time even (1 Cor 15:4-8).

As St. Peter puts it:

Prizing His Passion

> For we did *not* follow cleverly devised tales when we made known to you the power and coming of our Lord Jesus Christ, but we were *eyewitnesses* of His majesty. For when He received honor and glory from God the Father, such an utterance as this was made to Him by the Majestic Glory, "This is My beloved Son with whom I am well-pleased"—and we ourselves *heard* this utterance made from heaven when we were with Him on the holy mountain (1 Pet 1:16–18, italics mine).

Peter is referencing here his experience on the Mount of Transfiguration, where he saw Moses and Elijah—two key Old Testament figures who had departed this earth centuries earlier—show up supernaturally and converse with Jesus. Only he, James and John were eyewitnesses of *that* miraculous event, but they and thousands of other people witnessed countless other miraculous events during Jesus' earthly ministry. We can trust their testimonies and reports. We believers have a faith that fits the facts. It's historically and empirically true.

In a *Breakpoint* radio commentary early in 2017, Eric Metaxas mentioned that the magazine *Christianity Today* had recently run an article entitled "Biblical Archaeology's Top Ten Discoveries of 2016." Then he alluded to *Breakpoint's* coverage of such discoveries during 2016 and picked just three to recap. Here's what he said about one of those:

> Number two on our list of best biblical archaeological finds is the excavation of a "monumental pool from the Second Temple period, the period in which Jesus lived." In other words, the Pool of Siloam. You'll recall from John 9 when Jesus encountered the man born blind, he spat on the ground, made mud, placed it on the man's eyes, and told him to go "wash in the pool of Siloam." The finding is further confirmation that the fourth Gospel "rests on extraordinarily precise knowledge of times and places, and so can only have been produced by someone who had an excellent firsthand knowledge of Palestine at the time of Jesus." [2]

Even more exciting is *Christianity Today's most* significant archeological discovery of *2018*:

> The name of Pontius Pilate, the Roman procurator who interrogated Jesus and then ordered him crucified, has turned up for the second time in the archaeological record. The first time his name

---

2. Metaxas, "Real History, Toilets and All: Our Favorite Archeological Finds," *Breakpoint*, January 11, 2017.

6—Faith that Fits the Facts

and title were found engraved in a stone discovered in 1961 in secondary use at Caesarea Maritima. Just a few weeks ago [November 29, 2018], scientists announced that a seal ring excavated in the late 1960s at Herodium, a desert palace just outside of Bethlehem, also carried the inscription "of Pilates."

The inscription on the badly corroded ring was finally read using advanced photographic techniques. The copper alloy ring was probably not fancy enough to have actually been worn by Pilate. It was more likely worn by someone who was authorized to act on Pilate's authority and who would use the seal to create official communications.[3]

John Stonestreet explains:

Part of the significance of this discovery is *where* Pilate's ring was found: in the ruins of Herod's fortress, hence the name "Herodium." And so, we have physical evidence of two biblical characters carrying on in the way the New Testament tells us that they did. Another word for that is "history." Both the Apostles[4] and Nicene creeds assign Pontius Pilate a central role in the story of our salvation. He's one of only three people named in the creeds along with the Virgin Mary and our Lord. It's obvious why the latter two are in there, but why is Pilate included?

Because the reference to Pilate anchors our confession in human history. Jesus did not suffer, die, and undergo burial in some gauzy "once-upon-a-time," but in actual history on the orders of a real person who even left evidence of his existence. Unlike other religions, our salvation is grounded in history, and the restoration for which Jesus "suffered under Pontius Pilate" will also take place within history. In other words, Christianity is the real deal.[5]

I, for one, would not embrace it if it weren't. I suspect you wouldn't either.

---

3. Gordon Govier, "Biblical Archeology's Top Ten Discoveries of 2018," *Christianity Today*, December 27, 2018 brackets mine.

4. The relevant portion of the Apostles' Creed (in modern English) reads as follows: "I believe in Jesus Christ, his [God the Father's] only Son, our Lord, who was conceived by the Holy Spirit and born of the virgin Mary. He suffered under Pontius Pilate, was crucified, died, and was buried..."

5. Stonestreet, "It Go Boom: Sodom, Pontius Pilate, and Archaeology," *Breakpoint*, December 21, 2018, italics mine.

Day 7

WHO KILLED JESUS CHRIST? (PART 1)

Jewish deicide is a historic belief among some in Christianity that Jewish people as a whole were responsible for the death of Jesus. The anti-Semitic slur "Christ-killer" was used by mobs to incite violence against Jews and contributed to many centuries of pogroms, the murder of Jews during the Crusades, the Spanish Inquisition, and ... the Holocaust.

—WIKIPEDIA[1]

WAY BACK IN 1960, while I was working at Grand Sheet Metal, a factory in Melrose Park, Illinois, a young Mexican-American man of Roman Catholic background, asked me, "Who killed Jesus Christ?" That same year, while I was working at the same factory, a Jewish businessman from out of town—with a troubled look on his face—asked me the same question. Since then, various religious councils have wrestled with the issues and tried to free the Jews in particular from national blame in the matter.

Now it's well over half a century later and well over nineteen and three-quarter centuries since Jesus was cruelly mocked, brutally beaten, torturously crucified, and quickly buried in a garden tomb. But the question still

---

1. "Jewish Deicide," *Wikipedia*.

7—Who Killed Jesus Christ? (Part 1)

remains. *Newsweek Magazine*, in fact, raised it again in 2004 in an article by Jon Meacham entitled, "Who Killed Jesus?" It's a legitimate question, a good one, a profound one, and an inestimably significant one. It deserves an answer. So, who killed Jesus Christ? Who was actually responsible for His death?

First of all, it was the *Romans* (*Gentiles*) who carried out His execution. As the conquering and ruling nation, they alone had the power to inflict the death penalty. It was Pilate, the Roman governor and judge, who ordered the crucifixion of Jesus of Nazareth—in spite of the fact that three times he had declared Him innocent, in spite of the fact that he attempted publicly to wash his hands of His blood, and in spite of the fact that he had a sign affixed to the cross over Jesus' head which read, "This is Jesus of Nazareth, the King of the Jews." It was written in Hebrew, Greek, and Latin. In Latin it read, *Iesus Nazarenus Rex Iudaeorum*—INRI, for short, as we often see on symbolic crosses.

And it was a detail of Roman soldiers who whipped Jesus, stripped Him, dressed Him in a purple robe, planted a crown of thorns on His brow, mocked Him, spat on Him, beat His head with a reed, and led Him out to crucify Him, compelling Him to carry the transverse beam of the cross until, weakened from lack of sleep and the cruel scourging, He collapsed beneath the weight of it. It was they who drove the nails through His hands and feet and who divided His garments among themselves, casting lots for them. It was one of them who plunged the spear into His side after He had died, releasing blood and water from His pericardium and thereby clinically documenting the fact of His death. Quite obviously, it was the Romans who killed Jesus Christ.

But it was the *Jews* who delivered Him to Pilate. It was a Jew named Judas Iscariot who betrayed his master with a kiss and bartered his own soul for forty pieces of silver. It was the Jewish Pharisees, chief priests, and elders who, in bitter hatred and envy, plotted Jesus' death. It was the Jewish high priest Caiaphas who, without even examining whether Jesus' claim to be the Son of God could possibly be true, found Him guilty of blasphemy and tore his own robes in symbolical outrage. It was the Jewish king Herod who, along with his soldiers, treated Jesus with contempt and mocked Him, dressing Him in a gorgeous robe and sending Him back to Pilate.

It was a mob of Jews who clamored for Jesus' death and agreed to free Barabbas—a murderer, insurrectionist, robber, and public enemy. It was the same Jews who cried, "Crucify Him! Crucify Him! Away with Him! We have no king but Caesar!" It was the Jews who answered Pilate's protests by saying, "His blood shall be on us and our children" (Matt 27:25). And it has been. Jesus even told Pilate, "he who delivered Me up to you has the greater sin" (John 19:11). A human symposium, like Rome's Vatican Council II, can never absolve thousands of first-century Jews of their responsibility for the death of Christ. As a matter of unvarnished history, it was the Jews who, by proxy, killed Him.

But that gives no license to *anyone*, especially genuine followers of Jesus, to marginalize or persecute Jews in any way. As Chuck Colson has observed, "Jews have a legitimate concern about this. During the Middle Ages, Christians treated Jews terribly. In Russia there were pogroms against the Jews. And of course some of the maniacs around Hitler professed that they were killing Jews to purify the Christian race."[2]

Neo-Nazis and white supremacists still feel the same way about Jews. One of them, a man named Robert Bowers, burst into the Etz Chaim (Tree of Life) Synagogue in the Squirrel Hill neighborhood of Pittsburgh, Pennsylvania, during a baby-naming/circumcision ceremony on Saturday, October 27, 2018, slaughtered eleven worshipers and wounded two others (plus four responding police officers), repeatedly announcing his desire to "kill all Jews." According to the Anti-Defamation League, this atrocity was the deadliest attack on the Jewish community in the history of the United States. It was unspeakably horrific.

To put it mildly, all of these Jew-hating people have been—and are—horribly misguided. In reality, their blind hatred comes from the Source of all evil; they are motivated by Satan and energized by demons. Anti-Semitism—which, tragically, is mounting again in many parts of the world, including the United States—has absolutely no place in the heart of a true believer in Jesus Christ, who, during His sojourn on planet Earth, was, after all, Jewish. Actually, He still is.

Indeed, behind the movements of weak and wicked men, both Gentiles and Jews, was a superhuman being who engineered the plotting and implementation of Jesus' death. It was His archenemy *Satan* who killed Him. It was Satan who attempted to kill the toddler Jesus when Herod ordered the slaughter of all male children in and around Bethlehem less than two years after Jesus' birth (Rev 12:4, in connection with Matt 2:16–17). It was Satan who attempted to thwart God's plan of redemption by sorely

---

2. Colson, "Who Killed Jesus? Setting the Record Straight," *Breakpoint*, February 12, 2004.

7 — Who Killed Jesus Christ? (Part 1)

tempting Jesus in the wilderness just before He began His ministry (Matt 4:1–11).

It was Satan who entered into Judas when he had made his decision to betray his Lord (John 13:27). It was "the power of darkness" that enabled the chief priests, officers of the temple, and elders who had plotted against Jesus to arrest Him in the Garden of Gethsemane (Luke 22:52–53). It was Satan, working behind the scenes, who finally brought about his supreme desire on the dark hill of Calvary as Jesus died and was then buried in a tomb. As Jesus Himself said, Satan "was a murderer from the beginning" (John 8:44). It was Satan who killed Jesus Christ.

It was *Jesus Himself*, however, who deliberately went to the cross to die, who willingly laid down His life. Although His disciples repeatedly failed to comprehend and/or accept His prophetic words, He told them on multiple occasions that He was going to be betrayed, then apprehended, abused, and executed by the authorities, and that He was going to rise from the dead (Mark 9:30–31; 10:32a–34, e.g.). It was His primary reason for being on this planet. He did not, however, *have* to die. He could have asked His Father and instantly had at His disposal more than 72,000 angels to defend Him and keep it all from happening (Matt 26:53). Yet He willingly submitted himself to the awful ridicule, beating, humiliation, torture, agony, and, finally, death on the cross. No one could have taken His life from Him otherwise. He had said, "I lay down My life that I may take it again. No one [takes] it from Me, but I lay it down on My own initiative. I have authority to lay it down, and I have authority to take it up again" (John 10:17b–18, brackets mine).

In the Garden of Gethsemane Jesus had settled the matter when He said to the Father, "Not My will, but Yours be done" (Matt 26:39). On the cross, just before He bowed His head and gave up His spirit, He managed to utter the words (three in the English translation, but just one in the original Greek: *tetelestai*), "It is finished" (John 19:30)—indicating that He knew what He was doing and that His task was completed. According to the writer of the Epistle to the Hebrews, "He offered up Himself" (Heb 7:27). Don't misunderstand: Jesus didn't commit suicide; but He deliberately allowed Himself to be killed.

It's important to realize, moreover, that it was the will of *God the Father* for Jesus to die. As we saw on Day 3, according to the ancient Hebrew prophet Isaiah's reference to the sufferings of the Messiah yet to come, "The Lord was *pleased* to crush Him, putting Him to grief" (Isa 53:10, italics mine). Although the entire narrative surrounding that startling statement explains, some 700 years in advance of the actual events, the fact and meaning of Jesus' Passion, it's not the only Hebrew Scripture that predicts the ghastly details. Consider this excerpt from another one:

> I am poured out like water, and all my bones are out of joint; My heart is like wax; it is melted within me. My strength is dried up like a potsherd, and my tongue cleaves to my jaws; and You lay me in the dust of death. For dogs have surrounded me; a band of evildoers has encompassed me; they pierced my hands and my feet. I can count all my bones. They look, they stare at me; they divide my garments among them, and for my clothing they cast lots (Ps 22:14–18, stripped by me of its poetic structure).

In that this detailed description of death by crucifixion was penned centuries before that barbaric method of capital punishment was devised, let alone implemented, its application to the coming Messiah places it within the context of the great plan of God for the redemption of mankind. That plan, conceived even before the foundation of the world, centered in the bloody death of His only unique and dearly beloved Son on that sort of implement of execution (1 Pet 1:18–20).

What was the reason for the countless, bleeding, Old Testament, animal sacrifices if not to point to and find fulfillment in the Lamb of God who takes away the sin of the world? Peter announced plainly on the Day of Pentecost, fifty days after Jesus' crucifixion, that Jesus "was delivered over by the predetermined plan and foreknowledge of *God*" (Acts 2:23, italics mine). So, *God the Father* planned the death of His Son and was thereby responsible for it. In view of the Father's deep love for His Son, that's a startling statement; and, from all indications, it has an awful lot to do with His love for *you*.

Who killed Jesus Christ? There's one more vitally important answer to that question, and we'll consider it during our next time together.

Day 8

WHO KILLED JESUS CHRIST? (PART 2)

Was it for sins that I had done
He groaned upon the tree?
Amazing pity! grace unknown!
And love beyond degree!

—ISAAC WATTS[1]

WHO KILLED JESUS CHRIST? Who was responsible for His grossly unjust execution? As we've seen,

- A Roman procurator, a Gentile, sentenced Him, and Roman soldiers tortured Him and nailed Him to the cross.
- A Jew betrayed Him, Jewish religious leaders instigated His farcical trials and conviction, and those leaders stirred up a Jewish mob to clamor for it.
- Satan masterminded the plotting and scheming behind His death.
- Jesus Himself voluntarily permitted the whole thing to happen.
- God Almighty planned the event before the foundation of the world.

1. Watts, "Alas! And Did My Savior Bleed?" Verse 2, 1707 (public domain).

Prizing His Passion

But who *really* killed Jesus Christ? Who's *really* responsible for His death? *I* am! *You* are!

We are guilty of crucifying the Son of the living God! It was because of *our sins* that Jesus Christ ever had to leave heaven's splendor for earth's squalor and become a man. As we saw on Day 2, St. Paul put it this way: ". . . although He existed in the form of God, [He] did not regard equality with God a thing to be grasped, but emptied Himself, taking the form of a bond-servant, and being made in the likeness of men. Being found in appearance as a man, He humbled Himself by becoming obedient to the point of death, even death on a cross" (Phil 2:6–8).

But why did He do that? Because: "all [of *us*] have sinned and fall short of the glory of God" (Rom 3:23, brackets and italics mine). Because: "all of *us* like sheep have gone astray, each of *us* has turned to his own way" (Isa 53:6a, italics mine). Because: "the wages of sin is death" (Rom 6:23a). Because: "without shedding of blood there is no forgiveness" (Heb 9:22). Because He loved us: "God demonstrates His love toward *us*, in that while *we* were yet sinners, Christ died for *us*" (Rom 5:8., italics mine) In other words, He Himself bore "*our* sins in His body on the cross" (1 Pet 2:24, italics mine). "He died the just for the unjust, that He might bring *us* to God" (1 Pet 3:18, italics mine). He "released *us* from our sins by His blood" (Rev 1:6, italics mine). He was "pierced through for *our* transgressions; He was crushed for *our* iniquities; the chastening for *our* well-being fell upon Him, and by His scourging *we* are healed. All of *us* like sheep have gone astray, each of *us* has turned to his own way; but the Lord has caused the iniquity of *us all* to fall on Him" (Isa 53:4–6, italics mine).

As Francis Schaeffer has pointed out,

> The clearest example of the effects of the Reformation culture on painting is Rembrandt (1606–1669). Rembrandt had flaws in his life (as all people do), but he was a true Christian; he believed in the death of Christ for him personally. In 1633 he painted *The Raising of the Cross* for Prince Frederick Henry of Orange. It now hangs in the museum *Alte Pinakothek* in München. A man in a blue painter's beret raises Christ upon the cross. That man is Rembrandt himself—a self-portrait. He thus stated for all the world to see that his sins had sent Christ to the cross.[2]

I certainly can't endorse and approve everything that actor and filmmaker Mel Gibson has ever said or done (nor can I endorse and approve all my own

---

2. Schaeffer, *How Should We Then Live?* 98.

words and behavior), but when he produced "The Passion of the Christ," Gibson's own hand was "the one that put the nail in Jesus' hand—symbolic of the fact that he holds himself accountable first and foremost for Christ's death."[3] It's true: *we* killed Him. It was *our* sins that crucified our Lord Jesus Christ. *I'm* responsible for His death, and so are *you*.

We need to face this fact squarely and with the utmost sobriety. We need to see ourselves in the angry, mocking, jeering crowd shaking our puny fists at the bloody figure on the central cross on Golgotha. We need to awaken to the total innocence and unfathomable love of the One dying there and become incensed at the injustice of it all. We need to grab the person in front of us in the crowd, spin him around to confront him about his role in the whole atrocity, and realize . . . we're looking into our own face.

When St. Peter on the Day of Pentecost, in the power of the Spirit, convinced his Jewish listeners that *they* had crucified the Lord of glory and their Messiah, "they were pierced to the heart, and said to Peter and the rest of the apostles, 'Brethren, what shall we do?'" (Acts 2:37) Some 3,000 of them owned their guilt and blame, and so should we! They repented of their sins, cried out for forgiveness, and embraced the crucified, risen Jesus as their Messiah, their sin-bearer; and so should we!

---

3. According to The Premier International Fan Website for Mel Gibson's "The Passion of the Christ," FAQ, http://www.passion-movie.com/english/faq2.asp.

Day 9

WHAT JESUS EXPERIENCED ON THE CROSS (PART 1)

> *Pain insists upon being attended to.*
> *God whispers to us in our pleasures,*
> *speaks in our consciences,*
> *but shouts in our pains.*
> *It is his megaphone to rouse a deaf world.*
> —C.S. LEWIS[1]

THERE IS NO DOUBT in the mind of every reasonably well-informed person that a man named Jesus of Nazareth lived and taught in the land of Palestine some two thousand years ago. Not too many years ago archaeologists discovered the house where Jesus stayed in Capernaum. More recently, they discovered a boat that He may have occupied on the Sea of Galilee—or at least one like it. Still more recently, they discovered a synagogue in Nazareth where He probably taught.

Since there is also significant historical evidence of His crucifixion, neither is there any reasonable doubt that He died—probably on April 7, AD 30.[2] Nor is there significant doubt that He died by execution on a Ro-

---

1. Lewis, *The Problem of Pain*, 93.
2. There are several different views among Bible scholars regarding the date and the

9—What Jesus Experienced on the Cross (Part 1)

man cross, that He died by crucifixion. As Kenneth Woodward pointed out many years ago in a major article in *Newsweek*, "Unlike [the case with] some other religious figures, such as the Buddha, *how* Jesus died matters greatly to Christians. It would be a very different religion if Jesus had suffered a fatal heart attack on the shores of the Sea of Galilee."[3]

But He didn't; He was crucified—outside Jerusalem. The writer of a letter to his believing Jewish brethren scattered throughout the first-century Roman Empire decades later said that "Jesus, because of the suffering of death [was] crowned with glory and honor, so that by the grace of God He might taste death for everyone" (Heb 2:9, brackets mine). Not only did He taste it, He drank its cup to its dregs.

Well then, besides the obvious fact that Jesus tasted and experienced death on the cross on Golgotha, what else did He experience prior to His expiration? What did Jesus really experience on the cross that could make any possible difference to you and me nearly 2,000 years later? I want to suggest that He experienced—in a depth that we shall never completely fathom this side of eternity—three of the greatest problems of our technologically advanced generation: pain, guilt, and loneliness. We'll consider the first of those today and the other two tomorrow and the next day.

First of all, then, Jesus experienced *pain* on the cross. Plainly, He experienced the physical torture of crucifixion. He suffered unimaginable agony. Many years ago, Dr. William Edwards, an autopsy pathologist at the Mayo Clinic in Rochester, Minnesota (who had recently become a Christian), published a detailed medical reconstruction of Jesus' death in the *Journal of the American Medical Association*. According to UPI reporter Larry Doyle, Edwards concluded that

> ... the official cause of death may have been heart failure linked to asphyxia and other factors caused by the diaphragm-crushing suffocation of hanging on a cross and hastened by the gashing floggings and beatings he suffered before being crucified ... Roman crucifixions were designed to cause maximum pain to victims left

---

year of Jesus' crucifixion. The relevant historical data are numerous and are challenging to reconcile with certainty, but the most likely dates are April 7, AD 30, and April 3, AD 33. There are scholarly arguments supporting both dates. The later date (AD 33) would require that Jesus had a longer ministry than the Gospels suggest and that He began it later than they suggest. The earlier date (AD 30) would seem more consistent with what can be deduced about the start of Jesus' ministry from Luke 3:1, given its several historical references.

3. Woodward, "A Lesser Child of God," *Newsweek*, April 4, 1994, 49.

to exposure and slow death for up to four days, but Jesus did not live out the afternoon. He probably was in critical condition even before he was nailed to the cross, Edwards said. "Jesus' death after only three to six hours on the cross surprised even Pontius Pilate. The fact that Jesus cried out in a loud voice and then bowed his head suggests the possibility of a catastrophic terminal event. One popular explanation has been that Jesus died of cardiac rupture."

Before Jesus was executed, Roman soldiers first flailed him with a short whip made of leather thongs studded with pieces of sheep bone and small iron balls, Edwards said. The flogging would have shredded Jesus' flesh to the bone, leaving him in a pre-shock state from blood loss and near death . . . Once [he was at Golgotha], the dehydrated and exhausted man was nailed to the wooden planks by the wrists and feet with iron spikes 5 to 7 inches long that tapered from a square head shaft 3/8-inch across.

Edwards said his report was based on analyses of the Shroud of Turin, Jesus' alleged burial cloth, as well as both Christian and non-Christian historical documents. A rather graphic picture of what execution was like during the Roman Empire emerges from the evidence, he said. "There has been a tendency, by artists and others, to almost romanticize the crucifixion, to really try to disguise the horror of what Christ went through," Edwards said.[4]

Eighteen years later, in 2004, Mel Gibson released what turned out to be a block-buster motion picture called, "The Passion of the Christ," (mentioned on Day 8) perhaps the most graphic portrayal ever of Jesus' sufferings. Those who have experienced that production will no longer romanticize the crucifixion. Viewers uniformly left theaters deeply sobered, profoundly moved, and in hushed silence—saying little or nothing to one another.

But it's not merely a movie; it's historical reality. Jesus' flesh was brutally pierced and torn in several places, notably on His scalp, His back, His wrists, and His feet. His upper and lower arm muscles were horribly cramped. His pectoral muscles at the side of His chest were momentarily paralyzed over and over again. His nerves were agonizingly stretched like the strings across the bridge on a violin. His tongue and lips were mercilessly parched and thick. His lungs were gradually weakened to the point of sheer exhaustion.

---

4. Doyle, "Pathologist Examines Jesus' Death," *The York Dispatch*, March 22, 1986. The entire article in the *Journal of the American Medical Association* is currently available on the internet and contains much more detail.

9—What Jesus Experienced on the Cross (Part 1)

His entire system was inexorably drawn into deeper shock. His heart finally ruptured in a massive cardiac arrest. And, finally, His pericardium was viciously punctured, and both blood and water drained out. His face and body were beaten, bruised, and bloodied almost beyond human semblance, nearly beyond recognition by those who knew Him. He knew what it was to endure *excruciating* bodily pain—inflicted upon Him by the violent acts of other human beings.

It is possible, moreover, that in some supernatural way Jesus also experienced the gamut of physical illnesses and diseases as He hung on the cross. He may, in other words, have been unimaginably *ill* along with the wounds He sustained prior to and during His crucifixion. It's not hard to conjecture that He experienced a horrible headache and the onset of acute infection and high fever from the wounds He had sustained. But perhaps He also felt what human beings feel when they are afflicted with a non-injury-related illness or disease—the flu, pneumonia, cancer, malaria, multiple sclerosis, ALS, or one or more of countless other bodily maladies. I say that because Isaiah 53:3—in one rendering—states, "He was despised and forsaken of men, a man of *pains* and acquainted with *sickness*."[5]

Regardless of how we understand that statement, it is clear that Jesus can sympathize out of personal experience—as well as divine compassion and omniscience—with our physical pain, illnesses, injuries, afflictions, and suffering. It is clear, moreover, that He can heal us and make us well. For reasons that are sometimes difficult to understand, not everyone who seeks to be physically healed by Him today receives that healing. But in the first century it appears that *every* sick or handicapped person who came or was brought to Jesus in the Gospels or to His disciples in the Book of Acts *was* restored to health and wholeness.

For sure, one day every believer will be *permanently* healed—at death and supremely at Jesus' return and the great resurrection of the saints of all the ages! He is *Yahweh Rapha*, the Lord who *heals*, for He Himself experienced intense physical pain on the cross of Calvary. Please know that He understands *your* pain and cares for you deeply!

---

5. Young, *Young's Literal Translation of the Holy Bible*.

Day 10

What Jesus Experienced on the Cross (Part 2)

I get up and pace the room, as if I can leave my guilt behind me.
But it tracks me as I walk, an ugly shadow made by myself.
—Rosamund Lupton[1]

Yesterday we stressed that Jesus experienced pain on the cross. But He also experienced *guilt* as He hung there in unimaginable torment. He had no guilt of His own, because He had no sin of His own. Unlike you and me, He was *sinless* (can you imagine?) in thought, word, and deed. But, according to St. Paul, God "made Him who knew no sin to *be* sin on our behalf" (2 Cor 5:21, italics mine).

Since guilt in a large measure is an awareness of our separation from God and His holiness, coupled with an awareness of personal accountability and some sort of judgment to come, this is precisely what Jesus Christ experienced as He hung on the cross and became sin for us. Truly, "He Himself bore our sins in His body on the cross" (1 Pet 2:24) and now knows—far better than we—the reality of the consequences of sin.

For the first and only time in His entire eternal existence Jesus felt guilty; He felt the guilt of all the sins of the human race—past, present, and

1. Lupton, *Sister*, page unknown by me.

10—What Jesus Experienced on the Cross (Part 2)

future. For the first and only time He experienced total absence of communion with His Father. Quoting Psalm 22:1, He cried out with a loud voice, "My God, my God, why have You forsaken Me?" (Matt 27:46). For the first and only time He was punished for sin—not His, ours. He assumed the penalty, punishment, and judgment we deserve for our sin—eternal hell condensed into those hours during which He hung on the cross. He "died for sins once for all, the just for the unjust, in order that He might bring us to God" (1 Pet 3:18).

As noted on Day 8, "All we like sheep have gone astray, each of us has turned to his own way; but the Lord has caused the iniquity of us all to fall on Him" (Isa 53:6). The weight was unimaginably excruciating.

Strangely enough, the fact that Jesus was guilty of *no* sin qualified Him to become our substitute, to make Himself a vicarious sacrifice for our sins, to become the bearer of our guilt, shame, and punishment. And, equally paradoxical, what He experienced in terms of guilt, shame, and punishment prior to and then on the cross makes possible our freedom *from* guilt, shame, and punishment. As Paul put it, "There is therefore now *no condemnation* for those who are in Christ Jesus" (Rom 8:1, italics mine).

Many psychologists and psychiatrists have for decades tried to teach their clients and patients that they need to "get over" or deny or ignore their "guilt complexes" in order to recover mental health. Often, they prescribe heavy doses of tranquilizing drugs or even electro-shock treatments in an effort to erase, among other things, feelings of guilt. Nothing, of course, could be more foolish, misinformed, or counter-productive. Granted that there is such a thing as illegitimate, *false* guilt, there most assuredly is such a thing as legitimate, *true* guilt. And the Bible makes it clear that "he who conceals his transgressions will not prosper, but he who confesses and forsakes them will find compassion" (Prov 28:13).

After his horrendous sins of adultery and murder-by-proxy, David—confronted by the prophet Nathan—shamefacedly admitted, readily confessed, and thoroughly repented of them. In a psalm he wrote to express his confession and plea for mercy, he cried out, "Deliver me from bloodguiltiness, O God, the God of my salvation; then my tongue will joyfully sing of Your righteousness" (Ps 51:14). And he added, "The sacrifices of God are a broken spirit; a broken and a contrite heart, O God, You will not despise" (Ps 51:17). As Jennifer Turner points out,

> A "broken and contrite heart" is not taught in self-esteem workshops, and there is a danger that feeling the depths of our

sinfulness can lead to despair if we are not aware of the remedy available. What saves us is Jesus' cross, resurrection, and ascension—all three. [The writer of the Epistle to the Hebrews] calls this looking to Jesus, the one who has opened the way to God and continues to intercede for us.[2]

Consider, as well, these blunt words from the *New* Testament (some of which we previously contemplated on Day 4):

> This is the message we have heard from Him and announce to you, that God is Light, and in Him there is no darkness at all. If we say that we have fellowship with Him and yet walk in the darkness, we lie and do not practice the truth; but if we walk in the Light as He Himself is in the Light, we have fellowship with one another, and the blood of Jesus His Son cleanses us from all sin. If we say that we have no sin, we are deceiving ourselves and the truth is not in us. If we confess our sins, He is faithful and righteous to forgive us our sins and to cleanse us from all unrighteousness. If we say that we have not sinned, we make Him a liar and His word is not in us (1 John 1:5-10).

We *ought* to feel guilt whenever we sin; it's a valuable warning to deal with our sin before God and maintain a close relationship with Him. Thankfully, Jesus is the Lord who forgives and cleanses, because He experienced massive *guilt* on the cross of Calvary. Do *you* need to be cleansed of a guilty conscience today? Then come to Him in repentance and faith! "For if the blood of goats and bulls and the ashes of a heifer sprinkling those who have been defiled sanctify for the cleansing of the flesh [under the Old Covenant], how much more will the blood of Christ, who through the eternal Spirit offered Himself without blemish to God, cleanse your conscience [under the New one] from dead works to serve the living God?" (Heb 9:13-14, brackets mine)

---

2. Turner, "Confess and Be Restored," *Encounter with God*, Jan/Feb/Mar 2017, 71, brackets mine.

Day 11

What Jesus Experienced on the Cross (Part 3)

The most terrible poverty is loneliness and the feeling of being unloved.
—Mother Teresa[1]

During the last two days, we've wrestled with the pain and the guilt Jesus experienced as He hung on the cross of Calvary. But today we want to focus on the fact that Jesus experienced *loneliness* on the cross.

You'd think in the populous cities and metropolitan areas of *our* generation people would easily find and make friends and enjoy various forms of edifying companionship. But often such is not the case at all. Back in 1965, I wrote a leaflet entitled, "Who Cares?" It addressed the subject of loneliness. The American Tract Society printed and sold one million copies of it, other tract publishers "bootlegged" it, *Moody Monthly* and *The Pentecostal Evangel* printed shortened versions of it on their evangelistic page, someone translated it into Hebrew and published it in Israel, and stories of lives touched by it began surfacing. With its full-color cover photograph of the New York City skyline at night and its content about "the lonely crowd," it struck a nerve. People all over the country and even in other parts of the

---

1. Mother Teresa of Calcutta, "Mother Teresa Quotes."

world could relate to its message that simply articulated people's feelings of isolation and unimportance . . . and, thankfully, to the hope it offered.

Years later, things were pretty much the same. During Billy Graham's evangelistic crusade in New York City in the summer of 1991, before an estimated 250,000 people gathered in Central Park, he said New York was "the capital of the world" because of its ethnic diversity and its importance in fields such as business and the arts. "But," he observed, "with all of this overload of vitality and variety . . . New York City is a place in desperate spiritual need. Everybody I talk to, it seems, agrees that New York is the loneliest place in the world." "People," he added, "get increasing irritable and pushy in their effort to guard their own turf. There's little space for others, let alone God. To be without God in New York is to be terribly lonely." I heard him say these words. I was there, way at the back of that huge crowd.

Now we're well into the twenty-first century, and the problem still exists in epidemic proportions, in spite of internet-based social networking. Sometimes it even leads to suicide attempts, many of them deadly. Many people still "lead lives of quiet desperation."[2] Many feel that no one really cares about them. Even in the midst of a crowd, they know the pangs of loneliness. According to Julianne Holt-Lunstad, a professor of psychology at Brigham Young University, "Many nations around the world now suggest we are facing a 'loneliness epidemic.' The challenge we face now is what can be done about it."[3] British Prime Minister Theresa May, in an attempt to do something about it in *her* country, actually appointed a Minister of Loneliness on January 17, 2018, to grapple with the physical and mental health issues stemming from too much isolation. She said, "For far too many people, loneliness is the sad reality of modern life."[4]

Jesus experienced that. You remember the chain of events. One disciple had betrayed Him. Another had denied Him. Most of His followers had deserted Him. His enemies taunted Him. As Isaiah had put it prophetically some 700 years before Jesus' birth on earth, "He was despised and forsaken of men" (Isa 53:3). But then, as He hung on that cross and became sin for us, even His Father in heaven forsook Him. He was utterly alone.

Why? It all goes back to the sin, guilt, and punishment He assumed for you and me. We've been estranged from God from birth, due to the sinful,

---

2. Thoreau, "Economy," *Walden*, 6.

3. Downs, "Britain appoints Minister of Loneliness to tackle health problem 'worse than smoking,'" UPI, January 17, 2018.

4. Downs, "Britain appoints Minister of Loneliness . . ."

11 — WHAT JESUS EXPERIENCED ON THE CROSS (PART 3)

self-seeking bent we've inherited from Adam and Eve. Jesus *never* was estranged from His Father until that moment. His holy Father could not co-exist with sin. Jesus bore the guilt and punishment for our sin *all alone.* Listen to these words from His heart as He hung on the cross (expressed prophetically, and poetically, in a Hebrew Psalm penned by David): "But I am a worm and not a man, a reproach of men and despised by the people. All who see me sneer at me; they separate with the lip, they wag the head, saying, 'Commit yourself to the LORD; let Him deliver him; let Him rescue him, because He delights in him'" (Ps 22:6–8, stripped by me of its poetic structure).

He *had* to go through all of this. "Therefore," said the writer of the Epistle to the Hebrews, "He *had* to be made like His brethren in all things, so that He might become a merciful and faithful high priest in things pertaining to God, to make propitiation for the sins of the people. For since He Himself was tempted in that which He has suffered, He is able to come to the aid of those who are tempted" (Heb 2:17–18, italics mine). No wonder it meant so much to the Apostle Paul to have the Lord with him in *his* aloneness in Rome near the end of his life. Here's what he recounted: "At my first defense no one supported me, but all deserted me; may it not be counted against them. *But the Lord stood with me* and strengthened me, so that through me the proclamation might be fully accomplished, and that all the Gentiles might hear; and I was rescued out of the lion's mouth" (2 Tim 4:16–17, italics mine).

Yes, the Lord is omnipresent. Yes, He's promised to be with us always, even to the end of the age or, as the case may be, to the point of our physical death. But beyond that, He's been lonely Himself; He knows what it feels like, and He wants to extend to *you* His love, His care, His presence, His fellowship, and His friendship. As Paul declared, "I am convinced that neither death, nor life, nor angels, nor principalities, nor things present, nor things to come, nor powers, nor height, nor depth, nor any other created thing, shall be able to separate us from the love of God, which is in Christ Jesus our Lord" (Rom 8:38–39).

Allow me to recap our thoughts from these last three days. In spite of the tremendous advances in medical science, so many people today are ill or injured and are experiencing great discomfort and pain. So did Jesus . . . during His Passion. In spite of the best efforts of psychologists, psychiatrists, sociologists, educators, and even religious leaders, so many people today are ridden with guilt, separated from God, and ripe for judgment. So was Jesus . . . during His Passion. In spite of the best efforts of social agencies, religious agencies, and community activity planners, so many people today are all alone and lonely, often simply abandoned and forsaken by all others. So was Jesus . . . during His Passion.

So, if *you* feel lonely, don't give up! Don't despair! Turn to Him! He has walked this lonesome valley before you! He knows, He understands, and He cares!

Day 12

WHY CELEBRATE THE LORD'S SUPPER?

The Cross is the eternal expression of the length to which God will go in order to restore broken community.
—MARTIN LUTHER KING JR.[1]

I'M AN EVANGELICAL, AND most of us evangelicals don't usually think of ourselves as liturgically oriented, as being involved in a lot of religious rituals (although there's a movement afoot among some evangelicals to embrace the best elements of ancient liturgy and to make The Lord's Supper more central than it often has been). And yet, if we're honest, we have our own rituals. Chief among them are Water Baptism and Communion. Most of us try, however, to make our participation in those ordinances of our Lord as meaningful as possible, so they don't degenerate into matters of mindless rote. And, by the way, we typically call them *ordinances*, not *sacraments*—as others call them (although that, too, is starting to change in some circles).

In other words, we're doing them in obedience to our Lord's orders or commands; and, although we find them—or at least we *want* to find them—very meaningful, we don't view them as conveyers, in themselves, of spiritual substance or grace. We view them as *symbolic*. In the case of

1. King Jr., *Stride toward Freedom: The Montgomery Story*, 106.

Baptism, we see immersion in water[2] as *symbolic* of our identification with the death, burial, and resurrection of our Lord, as a vivid picture of the death of our "old man" and our newness of life in Christ (Rom 6:3–6; Col 2:12). In the case of Communion, we see the elements of the service—unleavened bread (perhaps broken-up matzo) and wine (usually grape juice, to avoid causing a recovering alcoholic or someone who might, unwittingly, be prone to alcoholism to stumble)—as *symbolic* of His bruised, battered, broken body and His precious blood, as a vivid, visual reminder of what He endured to purchase our redemption.

Depending upon their own traditions and convictions, some churches—especially those who consider Communion a *sacrament*—offer it every day . . . and at weddings (usually just for the bridal couple) and funerals. Some offer it every Sunday (or Saturday *and* Sunday). Some offer it once a month, usually the first Sunday of the month, and on special occasions like Maundy Thursday or Good Friday and/or Christmas Eve. Some offer it quarterly—four times a year. And some offer it just twice a year. Some include a foot-washing service as part of the experience.

All ecclesiastical leaders can tell you *why* they do what they do *when* they do it. But none can offer biblical proof for their practice, because Jesus simply said, "*Do this* in remembrance of Me" (Luke 22:19b, italics mine), and St. Paul simply added, "For *as often as* you eat this bread and drink the cup, you proclaim the Lord's death until He comes" (1 Cor 11:26, italics mine). Neither gave instruction as to *how often*, so there's a lot of latitude for differences on the frequency of celebrations of The Lord's Supper.

Thus, the issue I want to address today is not the frequency but the *motivation* behind our celebration of The Lord's Supper—*why* we participate in the religious ritual called Holy Communion. Let me say simply that the Communion Service, the observance of The Lord's Supper, or The Eucharist is a continual, visible, and tangible reminder of the efficacy of the death of Jesus Christ.

First of all, we partake of The Lord's Supper because it reminds us that Jesus' death has brought about *forgiveness*—the forgiveness of our sins. In

---

2. I realize not all evangelicals are immersionists; i.e., not all immerse baptismal candidates in water. Some sprinkle or pour water on their heads. Some totally spiritualize baptism and employ no water at all. The vast majority of evangelicals (including most Pentecostals, who now constitute one-third of the world's evangelical Christian population), however, practice baptism by immersion. That very statement is redundant, since the Greek word transliterated "baptism" actually means "immersion."

reference to the very setting in which Jesus instituted this ordinance, this practice, Matthew records:

> While they were eating, Jesus took some bread, and after a blessing, He broke it and gave it to the disciples, and said, "Take, eat; this is My body." And when He had taken a cup and given thanks, He gave it to them, saying, "Drink from it, all of you; for this is My blood of the covenant, which is poured out for many for *forgiveness* of sins. But I say to you, I will not drink of this fruit of the vine from now on until that day when I drink it new with you in My Father's kingdom" (Matt 26:26-29, italics mine).

He was telling His closest followers that shortly—actually the very next day—His blood was going to be poured out for many—including them—for the forgiveness of sins. It *was*—when His back was shredded by a cat-of-nine-tails, His scalp was lacerated by a crown of thorns, His hands and feet were nailed to a cross, and His pericardium was pierced with a spear. Remember: the writer of the New Testament Epistle to the Hebrews, in the context of his reflection on the Old Testament sacrificial system, made it plain: "without shedding of blood there is no forgiveness" (Heb 9:22).

But, as Paul explained, "In [Christ] we have redemption through His blood, the forgiveness of our trespasses, according to the riches of His grace" (Eph 1:7, brackets mine). As he also explained, "[God] rescued us from the domain of darkness, and transferred us to the kingdom of His beloved Son, in whom we have redemption, the forgiveness of sins" (Col 1:13-14, brackets mine). Pastor Gordon Cooke of South Wales has accurately prayed, "Lord, Your complete forgiveness is to be prized above anything else on earth."[3] For repentant and believing sinners, Jesus' death has brought about forgiveness—the forgiveness of sins, and every time we partake of it, The Lord's Supper reminds us of that.

We also partake of The Lord's Supper because it reminds us that Jesus' death has brought about *fellowship*—fellowship with God and with one another. We who have turned to God through Christ, trusted in Christ's atoning death, and received His forgiveness now have a brand-new relationship with God. We were enemies, strangers, aliens, foreigners, outsiders to His kingdom and family. But since Jesus has reconciled us to God through the cross, we're now friends, citizens, insiders, family members, subjects of God's kingdom. As Paul put it, "But now in Christ Jesus you who formerly were far off have been brought near by the blood of Christ" (Eph 2:13).

---

3. Cooke, "Look Both Ways," *Encounter with God*, July/Aug/Sep 2018, September 24.

But the fellowship brought about by the Lord's death is not just with God: it is also with one another—with fellow believers in Christ. Jesus said, "Drink from it, all of you." Paul wrote, "Since there is one bread, we who are many are one body; for we are all partakers of the one bread" (1 Cor 10:17). This means that *among those who are "in Christ,"* Jews and Gentiles are one, males and females are one, employers and employees are one, old and young are one, rich and poor are one, PhDs and high-school dropouts are one, blacks and whites are one, Hispanics and Asians are one, Republicans and Democrats are one, Pentecostals and Episcopalians are one, and Baptists and Lutherans are one!

I should add: in Christ, jocks and musicians are one! One of my two best buddies in college was a big-boned, six-foot, four-inch, 200-pound member of the varsity football team. I was a small-boned, five-foot, eight-inch, 140-pound trumpet-player in the marching band. Our spiritual lives intertwined on campus for four years and have, off and on, ever since. After the commencement exercises, we exchanged wallet-sized graduation pictures. On the back of my friend's he had written, "Thank God for the blood of Jesus Christ that made it possible for our fellowship in Him." On the surface, it sounds wonderfully spiritual, but I could wax a bit cynical and suggest that my buddy was saying, "If it weren't for the blood of Christ, there's no way we would have been hanging out with each other!" There's probably a lot of truth to that!

The fellowship at The Lord's Table in our local church should make us particularly conscious of our bond with each other. We should become keenly aware that we are one body, a significant manifestation of the visible body of Christ to our community. And our love and fellowship should far transcend that of normal human relationships. We're part of the New Covenant between God and His people. We belong to Him, and we belong to one another. No wonder Paul said, "But a man [or woman, of course] must examine himself, and in so doing he is to eat of the bread and drink of the cup. For he who eats and drinks, eats and drinks judgment to himself if he does not judge the body rightly (1 Cor 11:28–29, brackets mine). It's terribly important to have our hearts right before God *and* with our fellow-believers before participating in a service of Communion.

Why do we partake of Holy Communion? Because the Communion Service—the observance of The Lord's Supper—is a continual, visible, and tangible reminder of the efficacy of the death of Jesus Christ. His death has brought about forgiveness—the forgiveness of our sins. And His death has

12—Why Celebrate the Lord's Supper?

brought about fellowship—covenant fellowship with God and with one another. Each time we celebrate it, The Lord's Supper provides an opportunity to recognize, ratify, and renew the covenant! It provides an opportunity to bask in the blessings of forgiveness and fellowship! No wonder Paul said we should keep on doing it until our Lord returns: "For as often as you eat this bread and drink the cup, you proclaim the Lord's death *until He comes*" (1 Cor 11:26, italics mine)!

Day 13

WHAT THE SUFFERING SERVANT IS LIKE

*All God's plans have the mark of the cross on them,
and all His plans have death to self in them.*

—E. M. BOUNDS[1]

THE "SERVANT SONGS" ARE passages in the Old Testament writings of the ancient Hebrew prophet Isaiah that refer prophetically to "the Suffering Servant," the Messiah who was to come on the scene of human history—but not for nearly 700 years. In these passages the future Messiah speaks, and we learn things about Him that both confirm and enhance what we know about Him in the New Testament. In Isaiah 50:4–10, we learn about His tongue, His ear, His back, His cheeks, His face, and His God. Keep in mind that this is what our Lord Jesus *was* like during His brief sojourn on earth and, ideally, what we, if we're His followers, *should* be like.

What about His *tongue*—and ours? "The Lord GOD has given Me the tongue of disciples [of learners], that I may know how to sustain the weary one with a word" (Isa 50:4a, brackets mine). Because of His close relationship with His Father, He knew just the right thing to say to the needy person—the thing the Father wanted that person to hear and know; and

1. Dorsett, *E. M. Bounds: Man of Prayer*, 213.

13—What the Suffering Servant is Like

so should we. The Apostle Paul talked, too, about our tongue, our speech. Referring especially to believers' communication with fellow-believers, he said, "Let no unwholesome word proceed from your mouth, but only such a word as is good for edification according to the need of the moment, so that it will give grace [not grief] to those who hear" (Eph 4:29, brackets mine). Referring especially to believers' communication with those who are *not yet* believers, he said, "Let your speech always be with grace, as though seasoned with salt, so that you will know how you should respond to each person" (Col 4:6).

What about His *ear*—and ours? "He [the Father] awakens Me morning by morning, He awakens My ear to listen as a disciple [as a learner]. The Lord GOD has opened My ear; and I was not disobedient, nor did I turn back" (Isa 50:4b-5, brackets mine). Morning by morning, Jesus made a priority of spending time with His Father (who was invisible to Jesus then, as He is now to us) to hear what His Father wanted to share with Him regarding His love for Him, the plans He had for Him—even for that very day, and the things that were on His heart for those He would encounter that day. And Jesus not only listened and heard, He obeyed whatever directions His Father gave Him; and so should we. Even when He knew that the going was really going to get tough—to the point of the almost unbearable, He didn't yield to the temptation to turn back; and neither should we.

What about His *back* and His *cheeks*—and ours? "I gave My back to those who strike Me, and My cheeks to those who pluck out the beard" (Isa 50:6a). Because He didn't turn back, He let barbaric men beat Him mercilessly with a cat-of-nine-tails, shredding His skin and inflicting deep wounds on His back. Not only that, He let them punch him in the face and yank out by their roots many of the hairs in His beard, causing blood to trickle down from multiple pores in His cheeks and bringing great pain. As part of the Father's plan for the redemption of the human race, He made Himself vulnerable to the humiliation and agony of this sort of irrational and unjust treatment; and so, when the time comes, should we—for the propagation of His glorious gospel.

What else about His entire *face*—and ours? "I did not cover My face from humiliation and spitting. For the Lord GOD helps Me; therefore, I am not disgraced; therefore, I have set My face like flint, and I know that I will not be ashamed" (Isa 50:6b-7). Again, He allowed men to humiliate Him, even by spitting on Him in awful contempt; because He knew that this was part of His Father's plan. Because He knew who He was in relationship to

His Father, He suffered no loss of self-worth or self-esteem; in *His* mind, at least, He was not disgraced by this outrageous treatment and had no reason to be ashamed. And He set His face like flint;[2] He was determined to endure till the end—till His death on a barbaric Roman cross. Likewise, we should surrender ourselves to the Father's will and allow nothing to keep us from persevering until we've accomplished His mission for us on earth.

And finally: what about His *God*—and ours? "He who vindicates Me is near; who will contend with Me? Let us stand up to each other; who has a case against Me? Let him draw near to Me. Behold, the Lord GOD helps Me; who is he who condemns Me? Behold, they will all wear out like a garment; the moth will eat them. Who is among you that fears the LORD, that obeys the voice of His servant, that walks in darkness and has no light? Let him trust in the name of the LORD and rely on his God" (Isa 50:8–10). As Peter would later put it, "while being reviled, He did not revile in return; while suffering, He uttered no threats, but kept entrusting Himself to Him who judges righteously" (1 Pet 2:23).

He trusted in His God to vindicate Him—and God *did* . . . by raising Him supernaturally from the dead, by allowing Him to appear alive to hundreds of people, by taking Him back to heaven to His right hand of power and glory, and by making it plain that one day every knee will bow before Him and every tongue will confess that He is Lord, to the glory of God the Father (Phil 2:9–11). Paul offers a similar set of rhetorical questions and answers in Romans 8:31–39 and expresses a similar confidence in the impossibility of being separated from the love of God. We too need to realize that, though we may be marginalized and maligned now, we will be vindicated one day (2 Thess 1:5–10).

---

2. Flint was a well-known stone, a variety of quartz, an extremely hard, gray rock.

Day 14

He Loves Us

God loves each of us as if there were only one of us to love.
—St. Augustine[1]

Everyone in the human race longs for love. Everyone yearns for acceptance. And almost everyone cries out for freedom from the downhill drag of the built-in bent toward rebellion, sin, selfishness, and addiction. But not everyone *finds* love, acceptance, or freedom. That's because true love, authentic acceptance, and genuine freedom are found only in Jesus, the Christ. And the problems are (a) that not everyone has heard of Him and what He has to offer us humans, and (b) that many who *have* heard refuse to bow their knee to Him and receive what He has to offer *on His terms*. What are His terms? Repentance and faith.

What's repentance? It's a change of heart and mind, which leads to a change of direction, which—in turn—leads to a change of behavior and lifestyle. It's a heartfelt sorrow for sin, selfishness, rebellion, and failure to measure up to God's righteous standards. It's a renunciation of all false gods and all known sin in one's life. It's a readiness to experience the kind of change God wants to bring about in one's life.

---

1. St. Augustine of Hippo Regius, Annaba, Algeria, quoted in Commentary on John 3:16–21, Catholic Web Philosopher.

What's faith? Yes, it's an acceptance of the truths revealed in the Scriptures about God, about humanity, about Jesus Christ, and about you. It's a belief with the heart as well as the mind that God became a (medium-dark-skinned) human being in the person of Jesus of Nazareth, lived a sinless life in the Middle East, helped and healed countless people, made some fantastic claims about Himself, allowed Himself to be tortured to death, spilled His precious blood as an atonement for our sins, rose from the dead after His lifeless body was laid in a tomb, is alive today, and wants to invade our lives.

But it's also a personal invitation to Him to do just that, and it's a personal commitment of one's heart and life to Him. To believe, in the biblical sense, is to receive Jesus as one's Forgiver and to submit to Him as one's Leader or Boss. To believe, in the biblical sense, is to entrust one's life and eternal destiny completely to Him—to put all the eggs of one's life into His basket. To believe, in the biblical sense, is not only to believe intellectually that the elevator you're standing before on the first floor of a hospital or other high-rise structure is capable of transporting you safely to the seventh floor; it's to step into it, entrust your entire being to it, and ride it to that seventh floor.

But what will happen if you meet God's terms—if you repent of your waywardness and put your trust exclusively in Jesus, the Christ? Three things, among others. First of all, you'll find true *love*. Saul of Tarsus—once a fanatical, murderous, persecutor of the church of Jesus Christ who, as we've seen previously, later called himself the foremost sinner of all (1 Tim 1:15)—testified, "I have been crucified with Christ; and it is no longer I who live, but Christ lives in me; and the life which I now live in the flesh I live by faith in the Son of God, who *loved* me and gave Himself up for me" (Gal 2:20, italics mine)!

And John, once just a smelly fisherman from Galilee, in his description of the risen, ascended, and glorified Christ (whom he saw on the Isle of Patmos toward the end of the first century), said that He—"the faithful witness, the firstborn of the dead, and the ruler of the kings of the earth"—"*loves* us" (Rev 1:5, italics mine)! Why? For the life of me, I don't know. But He *does*! After all, as Paul declared, He "came into the world to save sinners" (1 Tim 1:15). He was justly accused of being a friend of sinners (Matt 11:19), because He loves the likes of you and me.

Second, if you meet God's terms of repentance and faith, you'll find authentic *acceptance*. Paul wrote that God has freely bestowed on us His grace "in the Beloved" (Eph 1:6). That means that once we're "in Christ"—in God's Beloved Son—we're *accepted*, we're included, we're family, we belong! And Peter said to us believers, "But you are a chosen race, a royal priesthood, a holy nation, a people for God's own possession, so that you may proclaim the excellencies of Him who has called you out of darkness into His marvelous light; for you once were not a people, but now you are the people of God; you had not received mercy, but now you have received mercy" (1 Pet 1:9–10). Is that cool, or what?!? You're the object of the affection and inclusion of the triune Creator-Redeemer-God of the universe!

Third, and finally, if you meet God's terms of repentance and faith, you'll find genuine *freedom*. Freedom from what? Freedom from sin! John spoke of "Him who loves us and *released us from our sins*" (Rev 1:5, italics mine). But can we break that down in order to understand it better? Sure. Jesus, first of all, has freed or released those of us who are believers from the *penalty* of sin—eternal separation from God in a place called hell, the garbage dump of the universe. It's true that one day all unrepentant people, both great and small, will cry out to the mountains and the rocks to fall on them to save them "from the presence of Him who sits on the throne, and from the wrath of the Lamb" (Rev 6:15–16). But, as Paul explained, "There is . . . *no condemnation* for those who are in Christ Jesus" (Rom 8:1, italics mine).

He has also freed or released us from the *power* of sin—from its grip on our lives. Jesus Himself said, "Everyone who commits sin is the slave of sin," but "if the Son makes you free, you will be free indeed" (John 8:34–36). Paul wrote, "For the law of the Spirit of life in Christ Jesus has set you free from the law of sin and death" (Rom 8:2). And the writer of Hebrews explained: "For since He Himself was tempted in that which He has suffered, He is able to come to the aid of those who are tempted" (Heb 2:18).

Furthermore, one day He will free or release us from the very *presence* of sin, as He takes us to be with Himself in that awesome place called heaven—first the intermediate heaven and eventually the permanent heaven on the New Earth. In that day, "He will wipe away every tear from [our] eyes; and there will no longer be any death; there will no longer be any mourning, or crying, or pain; the first things [will] have passed away," and He'll have made "all things new" (Rev 21:4–5, brackets mine)! One of the reasons He became a human being was "that through death [His death on the cross] He might render powerless him who had the power of death, that is, the devil, and might free those who through fear of death were subject

Prizing His Passion

to slavery all their lives" (Heb 2:14-15, brackets mine). There's no reason to fear death any longer when we know it will usher us into heaven, where there's no sin or any of sin's consequences!

As Eric Metaxas explains,

> "Dust you are, and to dust you will return," God told humanity when sin entered the world. If Jesus tarries, *you and I will die.* All of us. Accepting that is crucial to living a meaningful life. Even so, as the Apostle Paul wrote, death is "the last enemy to be defeated." Our longing for immortality is good! It was put there on purpose. We were meant—from the moment of our creation—to live forever. And the secret to eternal life *is* in Someone else's blood. But it won't happen the way some people think. That means Christians can accept death, knowing that He Who is the "resurrection and the life" has already defeated it.[2]

How does Jesus do all this? How does He free us from the penalty, the power, and one day even the very presence of sin? As Metaxas reminds us: "by His blood" (Rev 1:5). If you've seen Mel Gibson's epic film, "The Passion of the Christ," you now know—if you never did before—the meaning of "by His blood." You've seen the blood running down His face, His chest, His back, His arms, His legs, and His feet. You've seen it gathered in pools on the pavement in front of Pilate's judgment hall. You've seen it gathered in puddles at the foot of the cross. You realize, as never before perhaps, that "you were not redeemed with perishable things like silver or gold from your futile way of life inherited from your forefathers, but with precious blood, as a lamb unblemished and spotless, the blood of Christ" (2 Pet 1:18-19).

How does it work? I don't know. All I know is that from time immemorial, "all things are cleansed with blood, and without shedding of blood there is no forgiveness" (Heb 9:22). It's the price God has always exacted as payment for our sins. And only Jesus was qualified to make the ultimate and complete payment. "Now once at the consummation of the ages He has been manifested to put away sin by the sacrifice of Himself" (Heb 9:26). So, are *you* in need of true love, of authentic acceptance, or of genuine freedom? You can find all three *only* in Jesus Christ.

---

2. Metaxas, "Transhumanists and the Quest for Godhead: Momento Mori," *Breakpoint*, February 28, 2017.

Day 15

A Poignant Story from Bedouin Culture

*Either sin is with you, lying on your shoulders,
or it is lying on Christ, the Lamb of God.
Now if it is lying on your back, you are lost;
but if it is resting on Christ, you are free,
and you will be saved. Now choose what you want.*

—MARTIN LUTHER[1]

AILEEN COLEMAN, AN AUSTRALIAN missionary nurse who has served the medical needs of the Arab people of the Middle East for more than sixty years, told this poignant story to her longtime friend Franklin Graham. It's a true story that emerges from life in the ancient Bedouin culture. The Bedouin are descendants of Abraham's and Sarah's Egyptian handmaid Hagar and are often found speaking about "our great father, Abraham," who, like them, lived in goat-hair tents, as did Isaac and Jacob. The story took place in the southern part of the Hashemite Kingdom of Jordan near Wadi Rum, a bleak and barren desert area well-known to the Bedouin

---

1. Luther, Sermon on Nov. 3, 1539 on John 1:29, according to *Daily Luther Quote*, #187.

people and visited by my wife, my youngest daughter, and me in April 2004. It's recounted in Franklin Graham's book *The Name*.

> As two boys, Abdul and Mohammed, were climbing the rocky terrain one day, they wound up in a heated argument. Abdul struck and accidentally killed Mohammed. As with others of different races and cultures, the Middle Eastern temper has a very low boiling point. Most of the time, [Middle Eastern men] vent their volatile emotions with ear-splitting cursing, [with] flailing of their arms, and often with the flashing of gold-capped teeth. But this young man had lost control, and now his friend lay dead on the stony landscape, a victim of second-degree murder. Abdul experienced the ultimate horror. Looking down, Abdul's heart sickened as he saw the limp body of his friend.
>
> "Mohammed!" Abdul screamed. Mohammed lay strangely still, his neck twisted. "Mohammed, Mohammed!" Abdul shrieked, but Mohammed did not answer. Abdul shook him, trying desperately to get a response from his best friend. The lifeless body lay twisted on the jagged rocks. Abdul began to sob, the tears stinging his weather-beaten cheeks. Mohammed was dead.
>
> In Bedouin society, "an eye for an eye, [a] life for a life" still prevails. Knowing the inflexible custom of his people, this young man ran across the desert in terror until he spotted the sprawling tent of the tribal chief. The youth, gasping for air, raced to the shelter, grabbed hold of the tent peg, and screamed for mercy. When the sheik heard the boy's cry he came to the door. The young man confessed his guilt and asked for protection.
>
> It is a Bedouin custom that if a fugitive grabs hold of a tent peg and pleads for protection from the owner of that tent, if the owner grants protection, he will lay down his life for the one on the run. It is a matter of honor and duty; the integrity of the owner's name is on the line.
>
> The sheik looked at the frantic young man, his knuckles white from gripping the tent peg so tightly. The old sheik put his hand on one of the guy-ropes of his tent and swore by Allah. "Go inside," the sheik said to the boy with a wave. "I give you my protection."
>
> The next day, young men who had witnessed the crime came running toward the tent, shouting, "There he is! There's the killer!" But the old man said, "I have given my word." Now the boy's life depended on this old Bedouin's integrity. "Out of the way! Give us the boy!" they yelled. The old Bedouin sheik stood his ground. His name was respected in the village. His word was good. If these

15—A Poignant Story from Bedouin Culture

men, intent on revenge, laid a hand on Abdul, they would have to kill the old man first.

"Stand aside, sheik," a man yelled. "Give us the boy!" The old man stood strong. "No." His voice rang out as he slipped his hand around the knife hanging around his waist. "You don't understand," the pursuers argued. "That boy is a murderer. He has taken the life of another." "I've promised my protection. I will honor my oath," the sheik replied.

"Do you know who he killed?" the men argued. "It doesn't matter," the sheik replied. One of the men blurted out, "He killed your son—your only son!" The old man flinched as if a knife had pierced his heart. His eyes filled with tears. There was a long silence. The old man's knees weakened. His face tensed. On the floor of the sheik's tent, Abdul closed his eyes and buried his face, awaiting retaliation. Surely this was the end.

After a few moments, the old man softly spoke, "I'm an old man; I'll never be able to have another son." Abdul felt his heart race. *I'm dead*, he thought. "I have given the boy my protection," the sheik continued, "and I will honor my oath." "What?" The pursuers were stunned. "How can you honor your oath when he's the one responsible for your son's death?"

In a hushed voice the sheik said again, "I am an old man. I cannot bring my son back to life. Because this boy came to me in the right way, I will take him as my own son and raise him. He will live in my tent and will be my heir. All that I have will be his. He will bear my name."[2]

You and I are guilty of sin, and the punishment for sin is death. As fugitives, we have fled for refuge to the Chief of all chiefs, the true and living God. We have grabbed hold of the tent peg—the cross on which Jesus died. We have screamed for mercy, we have confessed our guilt, and we have begged for protection. The Chief has heard our cry and has given us protection. Even though we are responsible for the murder of His only Son, He has taken us into His family and raised us as His own sons and daughters (John 1:12). He has made us heirs of God and fellow heirs with Christ (Rom 8:17). All that He has is ours. As Paul asked, rhetorically, "He who did not spare His own Son, but delivered Him over for us all; how will He not also with Him freely give us all things?" (Rom 8:32)

No wonder the hymn-writer penned these memorable words:

> How firm a foundation, ye saints of the Lord,

---

2. Graham, *The Name*, 9–11, brackets mine.

Is laid for your faith in his excellent word!
What more can he say than to you he hath said,
To you who for refuge to Jesus have fled?
"Fear not, I am with thee, O be not dismayed,
For I am thy God and will still give thee aid;
I'll strengthen and help thee, and cause thee to stand
Upheld by my righteous, omnipotent hand."[3]

---

3. Robert, Richard, or John Keene, someone named Kirkham, or John Keith (authorship uncertain), "How Firm a Foundation," First two stanzas, 1787 (public domain), italics mine. Interestingly, the hymn was sung at the funerals of American presidents Theodore Roosevelt and Woodrow Wilson and at the funeral of General Robert E. Lee.

Day 16

Blood in the River

*Never did the church so much prosper and so truly thrive
as when she was baptized in blood.
The ship of the Church never sails so gloriously along
as when the bloody spray of her martyrs
falls upon her deck. We must suffer, and we must die,
if we are ever to conquer this world for Christ.*

—Charles Haddon Spurgeon[1]

You're aware, of course, that Jesus Christ, the Son of the living God, voluntarily laid down His life as an atoning sacrifice for the sins of the world. In other words, as the only One qualified to be our Substitute, He *died* for us. I want to remind you today that He also called His followers to be ready to lay down *their* lives. In other words, as those who claim to follow Him, we need to be ready to suffer ridicule, ostracism, persecution, incarceration, torture, and even death for our identification with Him. After all, Jesus said, "Truly, truly, I say to you, unless a grain of wheat falls into the earth and dies, it remains alone; but if it dies, it bears much fruit. He who loves his life loses it, and he who hates his life in this world will keep it to life eternal" (John 12:24–25).

---

1. Spurgeon, "Separating the Precious [from] the Vile," *The Complete Works of C. H. Spurgeon*, Volume 6, 1860, page unknown by me.

Prizing His Passion

In his book *The Church God Blesses*, Pastor Jim Cymbala of Brooklyn Tabernacle tells the story of Jay and Angeline Tucker, Assemblies of God missionaries to what was then the Belgian Congo in the heart of Africa. Like two of my heroes, Conservative Baptist missionaries Don and Peg Penney, they were serving during the Communist-inspired reign of terror in the early 1960s. Home in America for a much-needed furlough,

> . . . the Tuckers followed closely the news from Congo. Things seemed peaceful again, but they still felt a bit apprehensive about returning to Congo with three children. "I must go back," Jay told his wife one day. "God is calling me back. We must trust him. We have trusted him for twenty-five years. It must not be different now." So, in August 1964, the Tucker family returned to [the city of] Paulis.
>
> They received a warm reception from missionary friends and Congolese believers, but the city was already in a state of unrest. Rebel forces were threatening government troops in nearby areas, but everyone felt sure that they could never take control of Paulis. Just two weeks before the children were to be taken to boarding school, rebel forces did the unthinkable. They entered the city and brought death and carnage everywhere. Dead bodies littered the streets as the Tuckers anxiously waited for events to unfold. Jay was taken in for questioning several times, but he was always released safely.
>
> Soon things turned even more grim. The Tuckers' car was confiscated, and they were put under house arrest with soldiers posted outside their door. Jay was arrested on November 4, along with the dozens of others, and was held in the Catholic Mission. The rebels grew violent and began marauding through the streets. On November 24 a rebel band came to the mission and dragged Jay Tucker and the other prisoners out into the streets. Using mainly gun butts and beer bottles, the rebels hacked and clubbed the dedicated missionary and twelve others to death. It was reported that Jay's screams could be heard for blocks as the angry mob took some forty-five minutes to kill him. The next day his body was thrown back into the jungle, where his bloodied remains were tossed into the crocodile-infested Bomokandi River. Two days later, on Thanksgiving Day, Belgian paratroopers rescued Angeline Tucker and her three children and transported them out of Paulis . . .
>
> . . . When laid next to the doctrinal perversions of the "name it and claim it" prosperity teachers, the life and times of Jay Tucker

16—Blood in the River

certainly seem meager and wasted. But now, as they say, let's hear the rest of the story.

The Bomokandi River flowed through the Nganga region of Congo, where the Mangbetu tribe lived. The Mangbetus had remained totally resistant to any penetration of the gospel. Even the famous missionary C.T. Studd was never able to win one Mangbetu convert. Another mission group followed up on his efforts, but not one Mangbetu turned to the Lord.

As the Congo rebellion subsided, the king of the Mangbetus persuaded the central government in Kinshasa to send a chief of police to bring stability to the region. The government sent a man of strong stature who was known simply as "the Brigadier." What no one knew was that the Brigadier had been won to Christ by Jay Tucker a few months earlier.

The spiritual environment the Brigadier encountered was one of total darkness, and the relatively new Christian found no response to his first attempt at sharing the gospel of Christ. Then one day the Brigadier heard of a unique Mangbetu traditional saying: "If the blood of any man flows in our river, the Bomokandi River, you must listen to his message." This saying had been part of tribal culture from time immemorial. Suddenly a thought came to the Brigadier. He summoned the king and village elders to meet him at a designated place for a special meeting. They respectfully gathered in full assembly to hear what he had to say:

> *I want to tell you something. Sometime ago a man was killed, and his body was thrown into your river, the Bomokandi River. The crocodiles in this river ate him up. His blood flowed in your river. Now before he died, he left me this message.*
>
> *This message concerns God's Son, the Lord Jesus Christ, who came to this world to save people who were sinners. He died for the sins of the world; he died for my sins. I received this message, and it changed my life.*
>
> *Now, if this man named Jay were here today, he would tell you this same message. He's not here, but his message is the same. And because this is the message of the man whose blood flowed in your river, you must listen to my message.*[2]

As the Brigadier preached the simple message for which Jay Tucker gave his life, the Holy Spirit brought deep conviction. The light of the gospel began to finally shine through to the Mangbetus, and many were converted. Today in the Mangbetu region

---

2. The story of Jay Tucker is adapted by Jim Cymbala with permission from the archival files of the Assemblies of God World Missions Department in Springfield, MO.

in northeastern Zaire (formerly the Belgian Congo),[3] there are hundreds of believers and dozens of churches. They can all be traced back to the passionate missionary whose blood flowed in the Bomokandi River. His love for people led to his death, but in dying he brought the message of eternal life in a way he never could have imagined.[4]

Jesus bids us, too, in one way or another: come and die. Have *you* heeded His call?

---

3. It is *now* known as the Democratic Republic of Congo.
4. Cymbala, *The Church God Blesses*, 127–32.

Day 17

The Price of the Harvest

*Radical obedience to Christ is not easy; it is dangerous . . .
It's not comfort, not health, not wealth,
and not prosperity in this world.
Radical obedience to Christ risks losing all these things.
But in the end, such risk finds its reward in Christ.
And he is more than enough for us.*

—David Platt[1]

Never underestimate the price the holy, sinless, pure, and righteous Son of God had to pay to *purchase* eternal salvation for us dirty, rotten, lousy, no-good sinners. The Bible says Jesus was "oppressed" and "afflicted" (Isa 53:7), and it talks in the same chapter about "the anguish of His soul" (Isa 53:11). The writer of the New Testament book of Hebrews says, "In the days of His flesh, [Jesus] offered up both prayers and supplications with loud crying and tears to the One able to save Him from death, and He was heard because of His piety. Although He was a Son, He learned obedience from the things which He suffered. And having been made perfect, He became to all those who obey Him the source of eternal salvation" (Heb 5:7–9, brackets mine).

---

1. Platt, *Radical: Taking Back Your Faith from the American Dream*, 181.

What does that mean? Well, as Donald Burdick, my seminary professor of New Testament and Greek, explains in the *NIV Study Bible* and *NASB Study Bible*,

> The principal reference here is to Christ's agony in the garden of Gethsemane ... Jesus did not shrink from physical suffering and death but from the indescribable agony of taking mankind's sin on Himself. Although He asked that the cup of suffering might be taken from Him, He did not waver in His determination to fulfill the Father's will. His prayer was granted by the Father, who saved Him from death—[not through sparing Him the experience, but] through resurrection.[2]

I say again: never underestimate the price Jesus had to pay to *purchase* salvation for us.

But never underestimate, either, the price that *we*—His followers—will have to pay to *publish* that salvation ... to get the message out to those who have yet to hear and understand it, to sow the seed in anticipation of a harvest of new believers. Ponder the words of the Psalmist: "Those who sow in tears shall reap with joyful shouting. He who goes to and fro *weeping*, carrying his bag of seed, shall indeed come again with a shout of joy, bringing his sheaves with him" (Ps 126:5–6, italics mine).

What does this *mean*? Missionary professor Del Tarr, speaking to an American congregation, used a powerful illustration from West Africa—where he served for fourteen years with the Assemblies of God—to illumine these verses.

> I grew up in a preacher's home in the little towns of Minnesota and South Dakota. I spent most of my free time with the deacons' kids on John Deere tractors, International Harvesters, Cases, Minneapolis-Molines. I learned how to drill oats, plant corn, and cultivate. And never once did I see a deacon behave like Psalm 126 says. What was there to weep about at sowing time?
>
> I was always perplexed by this Scripture ... until I went to the Sahel, that vast stretch of savanna more than four thousand miles wide just under the Sahara Desert, with a climate much like the Bible lands. In the Sahel, all the moisture comes in a four-month period: May, June, July, and August. After that, not a drop of rain falls for eight months. The ground cracks from dryness, and so do your hands and feet. The winds off the Sahara pick up the dust and throw it thousands of feet into the air. It then comes slowly

2. Brackets mine.

17—The Price of the Harvest

drifting across West Africa as a fine grit. It gets in your mouth. It gets inside your watch and stops it. It gets inside your refrigerator (if you have one).

The year's food, of course, must all be grown in four months. People grow sorghum or milo in fields not larger than this sanctuary. Their only tools are the strength of their backs and a short-handled hoe. No Massey-Fergusons here; the average annual income is between eighty-five and one hundred dollars per person.

October and November . . . these are beautiful months. The granaries are full—the harvest has come. People sing and dance. They eat two meals a day—one about ten in the morning, after they've been to the field awhile, and the other just after sundown. The sorghum is ground between two stones to make flour and then a mush with the consistency of yesterday's cream of wheat. The sticky mush is eaten hot; they roll it into little balls between their fingers, drop it into a bit of sauce, and then pop it into their mouths. The meal lies heavy on their stomachs so they can sleep.

December comes, and the granaries start to recede. Many families omit the morning meal. Certainly by January not one family in fifty is still eating two meals a day.

By February, the evening meal diminishes. People feel the clutch of hunger once again. The meal shrinks even more during March, and children succumb to sickness. You don't stay well on half a meal a day.

April is the month that haunts my memory. The African dusk is quiet, you see . . . no jet engines, no traffic noises to break the stillness. The dust filters down through the air, and sounds carry for long distances. April is the month you hear the babies crying in the twilight . . . from the village over here, from the village over there. Their mothers' milk is now stopped.

Parents go at this time of year to the bush country, where they scrape bark from certain trees. They dig up roots as well, collect leaves, and grind it all together to make a thin gruel. They may pawn a chair, a cooking pot, or bicycle tires in order to buy a little more grain from those wealthy enough to have some remaining, but most often the days are passed with only an evening cup of gruel.

Then, inevitably, it happens. A six- or seven-year-old boy comes running to his father one day with sudden excitement. "Daddy! Daddy! We've got grain!" he shouts.

"Son, you know we haven't had grain for weeks."

"Yes, we have!" the boy insists. "Out in the hut where we keep the goats—there's a leather sack hanging up on the wall—I reached

Prizing His Passion

up and put my hand down in there—Daddy, there's grain in there! Give it to Mommy so she can make flour, and tonight our tummies can sleep!"

The father stands motionless. "Son, we can't do that," he softly explains. "That's next year's seed grain. It's the only thing between us and starvation. We're waiting for the rains, and then we must use it."

The rains finally arrive in May, and when they do, the young boy watches as his father takes the sack from the wall... and does the most unreasonable thing imaginable. Instead of feeding his desperately weakened family, he goes to the field and—I've seen it—with tears streaming down his face, he takes the precious seed and throws it away. He scatters it in the dirt! Why? Because he believes in the harvest.

The seed is his; he owns it. He can do anything with it he wants. The act of sowing it hurts so much that he cries. But as the African pastors say when they preach on Psalm 126, "Brothers and sisters, this is God's law of the harvest. Don't expect to rejoice later on unless you have been willing to sow in tears."

And I want to ask you: How much would it cost you to sow in tears? I don't mean just giving God something from your abundance, but finding a way to say, "I believe in the harvest, and therefore I will give what makes no sense. The world would call me unreasonable to do this—but I must sow regardless, in order that I may someday celebrate with songs of joy."[3]

That might mean parting with much more of your money for the cause of world evangelization than you ever thought possible. It might mean making a break with the future path others—including your parents—have urged upon you. It might mean parting with your self-oriented career plans—with the "American dream," if you live in the United States. It might mean ending a dating relationship with someone who does not share your passion for the harvest. It might mean remaining single, if you can't find a spousal candidate who shares that passion. It might mean interrupting another legitimate career to focus on personal involvement in the harvest. It will certainly mean leaving your comfort zone.

As I mentioned in yesterday's commentary, it did for two of my heroes, Don and Peg Penney, who served as Conservative Baptist missionaries in what was then known as the Belgian Congo during the 1950s before being forced out during the Communist-inspired uprising there in the early

---

3. Tarr, "God's Ways Are Unreasonable," *Leadership*, Spring Quarter 1983, 66–7.

17—THE PRICE OF THE HARVEST

1960s—only to retrain for outreach to the Wolof people in Senegal, where they served for the next thirty years.[4] I once heard Don tell of an experience he'd had in Congo while teaching tribal people about the death, burial, and resurrection of Jesus Christ—people who were hearing the gospel for the very first time. After he had mentioned that Jesus was crucified on a Friday, a tribal leader raised a question: "Bwana," he asked, "was that *last* Friday?" Upon learning, to his shock, that the events associated with the Passion had taken place over 1,900 years prior to that, the tribal leader asked another question: "Then why has no one come until now to tell *my* people?" Why, indeed?!? Oh, the failure of the church of Jesus Christ down through the centuries to reach *every* tribe, language-group, people, and nation!

If the Lord of the harvest uses that heart-touching, true story to challenge you about investing the rest of *your* life in the cross-cultural communication of the gospel where the church doesn't exist yet, and if you find yourself struggling with the changes you'd have to make to follow His call, just remember what Jesus said: "If anyone wishes to come after Me, he must deny himself, and take up his cross and follow Me. For whoever wishes to save his life will lose it; but whoever loses his life for My sake will find it" (Matt 16:24–25).

---

4. Since the Penneys were the first resident missionaries on Senegalese soil, there were virtually no Christians in that West African country when they launched their ministry in Thiès in 1962. According to pp. 730–32 of the 2010 edition of *Operation World* (the Seventh Edition), there are now 825,658 professing Christians in Senegal—77,800 of them evangelicals (including Pentecostals and charismatics). Sadly, there are only about one-hundred believers among the Wolof people and only the beginnings of a few congregations. Thankfully, several factors—including the availability of the entire New Testament in the Wolof language—indicate that a breakthrough could be on the horizon among that tribal group in whom Don and Peg invested three decades of their lives. Inspired in part by his parents' against-the-odds faithfulness in that predominantly Muslim country, Dan Penney and his wife Esther are currently missionaries there. They are involved in leadership development.

Day 18

How I Got In

Nothing in my hand I bring; simply to Thy cross I cling.
—Augustus M. Toplady[1]

THERE IS A STORY that comes from the days in which D. L. Moody was a great evangelist: Somewhere in the eastern part of the United States he was conducting a crusade in a large city auditorium. The building was filled to capacity well ahead of the service one evening, and not long before it was to begin, a dirty and ragged young street kid showed up, hoping to hear Mr. Moody preach.

> Just as he walked through the front door, a sexton spotted him and, noticing his appearance, came over, put his hand on his shoulder, turned him around, and said, "Son, you can't come in here the way you appear." Disappointed, the little boy went out, but he went around to another door and tried again to get in. This time when the sexton spotted him, he clasped him by the shoulder a bit more roughly, spun him around, and turned him out the door, saying, "You can't come in here; you aren't fit." Terribly disappointed, the little boy found yet another door and tried a third time to get in. This time, when the sexton caught him, he ejected him even more forcefully.

---

1. Toplady, "Rock of Ages," Verse 3, 1763 (public domain).

18—How I Got In

So he walked across the alley, leaned up against a stone wall, tucked his head down in his arms, and started to sob. He wanted so badly to hear Mr. Moody preach, but he couldn't get in.

Just then a carriage drove up and a large man got out of it and started for the hall; but, hearing the sound of sobbing, he looked around and saw the little boy leaning up against the wall. He went over, put his hand on the boy's shoulder, and said tenderly, "What's the matter, Sonny?" Through his tears, the little boy replied, "Sir, I came to hear Mr. Moody preach tonight. But I'm not fit. I'm dirty and ragged, and there's a rough man at the door who won't let me in."

The large man looked down with a twinkle in his eye and said, "Do you really want to hear Mr. Moody preach?" "Oh, sir," he replied, "I do." Then the man said, "Sonny, *I'm* going in that hall. If you were with *me*, the man at the door wouldn't stop you. But it's up to you. You're welcome to go there with me." With that, the man turned and strode across the gravel toward the hall.

The little boy dashed the tears out of his eyes, ran up behind him, and reaching out, clasped the only thing he could get hold of—the man's long frock-coat; and they stepped together into the vestibule. The sexton looked up, recognized *Mr. Moody*, bowed, and then, noting the little boy holding on to his coat-tails, watched in utter astonishment as the two walked down the aisle to the very front of the auditorium.

The man who told this story in Scotland years later insisted that it was absolutely true, because, he said, "*I* was that little boy." He continued, "I got in there that night, and I got to hear Mr. Moody preach, and I heard the word of God, and I became a Christian. And today I'm a minister of the gospel."

He said, "I got in simply because, though I wasn't fit, a man said, "*I'm* going in, and if you're with *me*, they can't stop you." And then that preacher looked at the audience in Scotland and said, "Ladies and gentlemen, when the time comes that you and I enter heaven, we will not be there because *we* are fit, but because another called Jesus stepped into our pathway and said, '*I'm* going over, and if you are ahold of *Me*—if you belong to *Me*, there's no power in earth or hell that can stop you [from getting in].'"[2]

---

2. Slightly-edited story related by Dr. Myron Augsburger, for many years a Mennonite evangelist and then President (1965–1980) of Eastern Mennonite College (now University) in Harrisonburg, VA, in a recorded sermon entitled, "The Cross and Forgiveness" (italics and brackets mine), no date.

The glorious thing about God's grace is that, although God knows all the dirty, rotten, filthy things we've ever thought, said, and done, if we see them as hell-deserving offenses against Him, confess them, and repent of them, He forgives us of them, cleanses us of them, accepts us into His family of holy ones, transforms us, and prepares a place for us in heaven. Think about it: in Jesus' body on the cross, God Himself has borne His own indignation at our sin and His own wrath upon our sin—wrath that should rightly fall on us (Rom 1:18; 2:1–6; 5:8–9).

So, please understand: *we can't make it without Him!* We can't make it on earth in *this* life successfully without Him, and we certainly can't make it into heaven in the *next* one without Him. After all, He said plainly, "I am the way, and the truth, and the life; no one comes to the Father but through Me" (John 14:6).

Day 19

SHARING IN HIS SUFFERINGS

*There are no crown-wearers in heaven
who were not cross-bearers here below.*

—CHARLES HADDON SPURGEON[1]

DURING HIS EARTHLY MINISTRY, Jesus often spoke not just of the fact that He was going to take up a cross, lug it to a place of execution outside the city of Jerusalem, and die on it, but also of the fact that, if we wanted to be His followers, we too would have to take up a cross and prepare to die on it—figuratively and perhaps even literally, whether or not crucifixion would be the method employed in our martyrdom. We saw that on Day 16.

Here's what Pastor John Piper says about it:

> Following Jesus means continuing the work he came to do—gathering a people in allegiance to him for the glory of his Father . . . Continuing the work he came to do even includes the suffering he came to do. Following Jesus means that we share in his suffering . . . And he knew that his own pain would also fall on those who followed him. "If they persecuted me, they will also persecute you" (John 15:20) . . .
>
> He did not die to make this life easy for us or prosperous. He died to remove every obstacle to our everlasting joy in making

---

1. Spurgeon, *Gleanings among the Sheaves*, 57.

much of him. And he calls us to follow him in his sufferings because this life of joyful suffering for Jesus' sake (Matt 5:12) shows that he is more valuable than all the earthly rewards that the world lives for (Matt 13:44; 6:19–20). If you follow Jesus only because he makes life easy now, it will look to the world as though you really love what they love, and Jesus just happens to provide it for you. But if you suffer with Jesus in the pathway of love because he is your supreme treasure, then it will be apparent to the world that your heart is set on a different fortune than theirs. This is why Jesus demands that we deny ourselves and take up our cross and follow him.

Of course, the pain is temporary. He does not call us to eternal suffering. That's what he rescues us from. "Whoever loves his life loses it, and whoever hates his life *in this world* will keep it for *eternal life*" (John 12:25). "Whoever loses his life for my sake and the gospel's will *save* it" (Mark 9:35). Suffering for Jesus is temporary. Pleasure in Jesus is eternal. When Peter said (perhaps with a tinge of self-pity), "See, we have left everything and followed you," Jesus responded without coddling Peter's self-pity, "Everyone who has left houses or brothers or sisters or father or mother or children or lands, for my name's sake, will receive a hundredfold and will inherit eternal life" (Matt 19:27, 29). In other words, there is no ultimate sacrifice in following Jesus. "You will be repaid at the resurrection of the just" (Luke 14:14). "Your reward is great in heaven" (Matt 5:12).

Even before heaven, joy abounds along the hard road that leads through death to resurrection. Nothing can compare with the joy of walking in the light with Jesus as opposed to walking in the darkness without him . . . Jesus promised, "I am with you always, to the end of the age" (Matt 28:20). And where Jesus is present there is joy—joy in sorrow for now, but joy nevertheless. "These things I have spoken to you, that my joy may be in you, and that your joy may be full" (John 15:11).[2]

After Saul of Tarsus was "arrested" and blinded by the risen, ascended Christ on the road to Damascus, the Lord appeared to a disciple in that city named Ananias and commanded him to go to the house where Saul was temporarily staying, to lay hands on him for the healing of his blindness and to baptize him in water. Then the Lord added, "Go, for he is a chosen instrument of Mine, to bear My name before the Gentiles and kings

---

2. Piper, *What Jesus Demands from the World*, 70–72.

19—Sharing in His Sufferings

and the sons of Israel; for I will show him *how much he must suffer* for My name's sake" (Acts 9:10–16, italics mine).

Jesus pulled no punches; He made it clear from the start that Saul, the former persecutor, would himself *be* persecuted as he traversed the Roman Empire to proclaim the gospel he'd just embraced. That is indeed how his life unfolded. No wonder he concluded his testimony to the believers at Philippi with this verbal crescendo: ". . . that I may know Him and the power of His resurrection and *the fellowship of His sufferings*, being conformed to His death; in order that I may attain to the resurrection from the dead" (Phil 3:10, italics mine)!

As reported in 2006,

> Diana grew up in a strict Islamic family in Pakistan. According to *Voice of the Martyrs*, her life was pretty typical until she met a girl named Mary who was a Christian. Now Diana is also a Christian and on the run. When Diana's family learned that she had become a Christian, they repeatedly beat her and insisted she return to Islam. But Diana refused. She was then forced to a local canal where her uncle put a pistol to her head and gave her one last chance to return to Islam. Diana replied, "You can kill me if you want. I will not leave Christ."
>
> It was then that Diana's uncle noticed an extremely poisonous black cobra swimming in the canal. Believing he could escape any prosecution for his niece's death, he threw her into the path of the cobra. He also knew she could not swim. Diana miraculously escaped from the canal and is in hiding today. She is a new Christian but has already learned what it means to suffer for Christ. She . . . told *The Voice of the Martyrs*, "Jesus was crucified for us. Can we not endure some of the same for Him?"[3]

This report, to say nothing of the 2015 video of ISIS terrorists decapitating twenty-one Egyptian Coptic Christians on the shore of the Mediterranean Sea near Tripoli, Libya, may sound strange or surprising to us. But why? Have we not paid attention to the predictions and promises of our Lord? Have we not read John's words? He wrote, "'*Do not be surprised*, brethren, if the world hates you" (1 John 3:13, italics mine). Have we not read Peter's words? He wrote:

> Beloved, *do not be surprised* at the fiery ordeal among you, which comes upon you for your testing, as though some strange thing were happening to you; but to the degree that you share the

---

3. From *Religion Today Summaries*, August 31, 2006.

> sufferings of Christ, keep on rejoicing, so that also at the revelation of His glory you may rejoice with exultation. If you are reviled for the name of Christ, you are blessed, because the Spirit of glory and of God rests on you.
>
> Make sure that none of you suffers as a murderer, or thief, or evildoer, or a troublesome meddler; but if anyone suffers as a Christian, he is not to be ashamed, but is to glorify God in this name. For it is time for judgment to begin with the household of God; and if it begins with us first, what will be the outcome for those who do not obey the gospel of God? . . . Therefore, those also who suffer according to the will of God shall entrust their souls to a faithful Creator in doing what is right (1 Pet 4:12–19, italics mine).

The author of the New Testament book of Hebrews states that "it was fitting for Him [God the Father], for whom are all things, and through whom are all things, in bringing many sons to glory, to perfect the author of their salvation [Jesus] through sufferings" (Heb 2:10, brackets mine). If Jesus, who was without sin, needed somehow to be perfected through suffering in order to fulfill His mission on earth, how much more do we, who are such sinful creatures, need to experience suffering as part of our spiritual growth process?

So, we should *expect* to share in the sufferings of our Lord, to receive the same kind of treatment He received here on earth. How soon do you think real persecution will break out in the United States of America (or, if you're not a US citizen or resident, in *your* country), if it hasn't already? When it does, will you be ready to take your stand for Jesus, for the gospel, for truth, and for righteousness? And will you be able to maintain your stand?

You may find yourself asking, "How?" May I suggest: by keeping your eyes on Jesus! By remembering what He suffered for you! By "consider[ing] Him who has endured such hostility by sinners against Himself, so that you will not grow weary and lose heart" (Heb 12:3, brackets mine)! If you've had a chance to read the book by Romanian pastor Richard Wurmbrand, entitled, *Tortured for Christ* (originally released in 1967), or experience the motion picture (released in 2018) by the same title and based on the book, you have new insight into the horrific nature of demonically inspired persecution—in this case, under Communism—*and* the supernatural work of God in the hearts of His servants that enables them to withstand such atrocities and even to love and forgive their persecutors.

Food for sober thought . . . and radical commitment.

Day 20

Dying Daily

When the time comes to die, make sure that all you have to do is die!
—*Jim Elliot*[1]

In a somewhat obscure and enigmatic section of chapter 15 of 1 Corinthians, the apostle Paul writes, "I affirm, brethren, by the boasting in you which I have in Christ Jesus our Lord, I die daily" (v. 31). As you can see, he bluntly states, "I die daily." What is he talking about?

Was he terminally ill? We have no record of that. Was he promulgating a "deeper life" message about death to "self"? Although he did speak in Romans 6 about our "old self" being "crucified with" Christ (v. 6) and the need to consider ourselves "to be dead to sin" (v. 11), the context in 1 Corinthians indicates no such thing. Was he pathologically paranoid—convinced that sinister enemies were out to get him and that any day now they might succeed? Perhaps—in a way, but there's no evidence of irrational fear, delusional visions, or unnecessarily impulsive behavior on his part.

What then? We need to examine the context. Here's the whole paragraph:

> Otherwise, what will those do who are baptized for the dead? If the dead are not raised at all, why then are they baptized for them? Why are we also in danger every hour? I affirm, brethren, by the

---

1. Elisabeth Elliot, *Through Gates of Splendor*, 253.

boasting in you which I have in Christ Jesus our Lord, I die daily. If from human motives I fought with wild beasts at Ephesus, what does it profit me? If the dead are not raised, LET US EAT AND DRINK, FOR TOMORROW WE DIE.[2] Do not be deceived: "Bad company corrupts good morals."[3] Become sober-minded as you ought, and stop sinning; for some have no knowledge of God. I speak this to your shame (1 Cor 15:19–23).

At first glance, the mysterious question at the outset of the paragraph seems to exacerbate the problem of understanding Paul's statement in verse 31, not solve it. What is this about baptism for the dead? Does it suggest a proxy baptism for dead friends, loved ones, and ancestors, as practiced by our Mormon friends? I don't believe this solitary (and passing) reference to the subject should give rise to such an interpretation.

Isn't it more likely that Paul is assuming that, as new believers are being baptized upon their profession of faith in Jesus Christ, they are filling the ranks of believers who have already died? Isn't he simply documenting the truth of Jesus' statement about His church that "the gates of Hades [the abode of departed spirits, containing—at the time He said this prior to His death, burial, resurrection, and ascension—sections for both the saved and the lost] will not overpower it"?

Remember: the whole context of this chapter is Paul's defense of both the historical fact and the practical importance of the literal, bodily resurrection of Jesus Christ from the dead. Thus, he's asking, if there is no such thing as the resurrection from the dead,

- Why are new believers being baptized to fill the ranks of departed ones (v. 29)?
- Why are we also in danger every hour (v. 30)?
- Why have I fought with wild beasts at Ephesus (v. 32)?

He's saying that if there's no future resurrection, it's all pointless, useless, and even ridiculous—an exercise in futility. Of course, he doesn't for a moment believe that. As a former Pharisee, he has always believed in the ultimate resurrection of the dead, and as a follower now of Jesus who has actually seen *Him* alive from the dead, he's convinced of the reality of resurrection.

---

2. This is an Old Testament quotation from Isaiah 22:13, emphasized in the *NASB* by capital letters.

3. This is a quotation from the Greek comedy *Thais*, which was written by the Greek poet Menander, whose writings would have been familiar to the Corinthians.

20—Dying Daily

In fact, he's so adamant about its reality that he believes anyone among his letter's recipients who *doesn't* has been deceived and allowed skeptics to corrupt his or her previously good morals. He's so unshakable in his confidence in its reality that he feels believers' failure to communicate "the knowledge of God" is both sinful and shameful.

It's in this context that He testifies to having "fought with wild beasts at Ephesus." Whether he means he had a literal battle with wild animals (perhaps in a gladiatorial arena, although, as a Roman citizen, he would not—or at least should not—have been compelled so to fight) or a figurative one with false teachers (like "the savage wolves" to whom he alluded in his farewell address to the Ephesian elders in Acts 20:29) is immaterial. The point is the same: if there is no resurrection (which some were suggesting), then why regularly put oneself in mortal danger from religious or political authorities by preaching the gospel of Christ? Not only that, but if there is no resurrection, there is no gospel to preach; for the gospel affirms that "Christ died for our sins according to the [Hebrew] Scriptures, and that He was buried, and that He was *raised* on the third day according to the Scriptures, and that He appeared [alive from the dead] to Cephas [Peter], then to the twelve [original apostles]" (1 Cor 15:1-5, italics and brackets mine).

So, here's the deal: Paul was in danger of persecution, arrest, abuse, torture, and even death every hour of every day of his life as a follower of Christ. Just read his reference to a near-death experience in Asia Minor in 2 Corinthians 1:8-10 and his list of dangers and painful experiences in 2 Corinthians 11:23-27. Thus, in a very real sense he could say, "I die daily." I believe he was saying, in other words, "My testimony for Christ puts me at daily risk of life and limb; I have to be ready to suffer and even die for Him every day of my life. I cannot count my life as dear to myself. My driving purpose in life cannot be simply to survive—to stay alive at all costs, to perpetuate my earthly existence."

What, then, does this mean for *us*, if we're Christ-followers? If we're living under actual persecution for our faith, it means exactly what it did for Paul. But even if overt persecution has not yet come our way, shouldn't the bottom line be the same: we need to live each day on this troubled earth as if it were our last. Isn't it true that we really don't know when our earthly lives are going to end? Even if we've been diagnosed with a terminal illness, we still don't know exactly when we're going to die. Again, therefore, we should die daily; we should live each day as if it were our last.

But what are the implications of a statement like that? There are many:

- We should keep our relationships free from bitterness and resentment; we should choose to forgive those who have hurt us, no matter how deeply (Eph 4:30–32).
- We should make sure our loved ones *know* we love them, both by our actions and by our words (Eph 5:25, 33; Col 3:19; Titus 2:4).
- We should put our affairs in order—finances, wills, trusts, powers-of-attorney, living wills, funeral plans, etc.
- We should evaluate our daily and weekly activities to make sure we're actually "making the most of [our] time" (Eph 5:16, brackets mine) in the light of eternity.
- We should, in other words, make our top priority the kingdom of God—its growth and expansion; we should involve ourselves in some way in global evangelization (Matt 6:33; 28:18–20) . . . by going ourselves (whether short-term or long-term), by our financial support of those on the front lines (Phil 4:15–19), and/or by pointed intercession for those very people (Col 4:2) and for the overall cause (Matt 9:36–38)—the world's and history's greatest.
- We should let our light so shine before those around us that they will see our good deeds and give glory to our Father in heaven because of them (Matt 5:16).
- We should seek opportunities to share the gospel as accurately and as winsomely as we can with those whom God has placed in our immediate surroundings—our neighborhood, our workplace, our school, our teams, our social circles (Col 4:5–6).
- We should do everything we can to help populate heaven (Matt 6:19–21; Phil 4:1).
- In other words, we should make the rest of our life here on earth really count—for heaven's sake (literally)!

Thus, if you grasp what I'm trying to say, to "die daily" is not at all a negative thing—a downer, a bummer. Quite the reverse: it's the most positive, uplifting, liberating thing imaginable! "Dying," in this sense, makes life worth living!

Day 21

FORGIVENESS—AMISH-STYLE

Forgiveness is an act of the will, and the will can function regardless of the temperature of the heart.

—CORRIE TEN BOOM[1]

As former residents of York County, Pennsylvania, my wife and I used to live not far from the Amish communities of Lancaster County. We often heard talk of Amish-style potato salad, Amish-style macaroni salad, Amish-style crafts, Amish-style quilts, Amish-style farms—without most modern conveniences, Amish-style lighting—by candle and lantern, and Amish-style transportation—by horse and buggy. Indeed, when traveling through Lancaster County for various reasons, we often saw those horses and buggies.

There are many aspects of Amish life and religion with which we twenty-first-century evangelical Christians do not agree, but—coming from a biblical perspective and worldview—we *ought* to agree with Amish-style *forgiveness*. You may recall the horrific event that took place in Nickel Mines, a village in Bart Township of Lancaster County, on October 2, 2006. I vividly remember it playing out on local and national television. A demented gunman, Charles Carl Roberts IV, took a room full of Amish

---

1. ten Boom, "Corrie ten Boom on Forgiveness," *Guideposts*, November 1972, page unknown by me.

school-girls hostage and eventually shot and killed five of them (ages six to thirteen) in cold blood before taking his own life.

"But as shocking as this senseless act of violence was," as Chuck Colson pointed out a year later, "it was what followed that sent the real shock waves through the nation." He went on to recall what happened next:

> Within hours of the shooting, several members of the Amish community visited Mrs. Roberts and her family, to express their sorrow over her loss and to say they did not hold anything against them. Another Amish man visited the killer's father. A Roberts family spokesperson said, "He stood there for an hour, and held [Mr. Roberts] in his arms and said, 'We forgive you.'"
>
> Four days later at the killer's burial, some 70 people in attendance were Amish. And when funds began pouring in for victims after the shooting, the Nickel Mines [Amish] community established a fund for the shooter's wife and children.
>
> Reactions to the news of this forgiveness ran the gamut from awestruck to disgust. Detractors like Jeff Jacoby opined in the *Boston Globe*, "I cannot see how the world is made a better place by assuring someone who would do terrible things that he will be readily forgiven afterward."
>
> But what Jacoby and others missed was the broader context of the forgiveness. It was not a cheap forgiveness that denied the pain and wrong of what had happened. From amazing grief through amazing faith came amazing grace.
>
> In a new book titled *Amish Grace*, three experts on the Amish explain, "Our actions are rarely random. We all embrace patterns of behavior and habits of mind that shape what we do in a given situation." As the authors note, there are "habits of forgiveness" in the Amish culture, Christian habits that come into clear focus. For instance, the Amish celebrate communion only twice a year, but they go through a month-long season of preparation. During that season of preparation, the Amish take seriously the admonition that if anyone holds a grudge against his brother, he is not to partake in the communion until he has put things right. A council meeting two weeks prior to communion is a time of admonishment, then there is a season of fasting, and sometimes the communion service is even delayed for weeks if there is more widespread disharmony among the community.
>
> So . . . the question is: how are we working in our own communities to build cultures of grace? Do we teach our children to forgive? Are we actively working to restore offenders and to reach

21—FORGIVENESS—AMISH-STYLE

out in aid to victims? And are we overcoming the evil in the world by good, as we are commanded to?

The Amish have given us a great lesson in the way to defeat hatred and alienation. It is the Christian worldview—the only one that makes such a magnificent response to such a horrible tragedy possible.[2]

It's that same worldview that made possible the almost instantaneous forgiveness of the murderer of *their* loved ones by the family members of the nine victims in the equally senseless massacre at the Emanuel African Methodist Episcopal Church in Charleston, South Carolina, on June 17, 2015. Their equally gracious words astonished a jaded press and nation.[3]

It's that same worldview that made possible the equally astonishing forgiveness of the murderer of his fourteen-year-old daughter and twenty-five other members of his congregation, the First Baptist Church of Sutherland Springs, Texas, on November 5, 2017, by Pastor Frank Pomeroy. That mass shooting, the deadliest in Texas history, also injured twenty other congregants before the perpetrator was shot by a civilian who lived nearby. After a high-speed car chase, the wounded perpetrator lost control of his vehicle, came to an unplanned stop, and killed himself. At the congregation's emotion-laden, first worship service after the massacre, Pastor Pomeroy—in an amazing display of grace—preached a message of forgiveness.

All of this, as we saw on Day 19, flows from Jesus' teaching about and model of forgiveness. Remember: as He hung in unimaginable agony on that Roman cross, He prayed, "Father, forgive them, for they do not know what they are doing" (Luke 23:34). And He laid down His life there as an atonement for your sins and mine. He let men spill His precious blood in order to make possible that forgiveness from the holy God of the universe. "To Him who loves us and released us from our sins by His blood . . . be the glory and the dominion forever and ever. Amen" (Rev 1:5–6).

---

2. Colson, "The Context of Forgiveness: Grace in Amish Country," *Breakpoint*, October 3, 2007.

3. On January 11, 2017, Dylann Roof, the mass murderer, was formally sentenced to death for his crimes.

Day 22

Donating Blood to an Enemy

Law and grace, life and death,
as well as time and eternity all intersect at the cross;
displaying a divine wisdom that staggers the imagination
and leads the humble heart to bow in thankful adoration.
To understand the cross of Christ is to understand
the heart of God toward a fallen world He wants to save.

—Steven Cook[1]

In the year 2007, the military forces of America and its partners were still waging a boots-on-the-ground war with Islamic extremists in Iraq and Afghanistan. On March 6 of that year, Chuck Colson said on his *Breakpoint* radio program,

> In Baghdad yesterday, a terrorist blew himself up with a car bomb, killing at least twenty-eight people and wounding dozens more. One witness told the Associated Press that pieces of human flesh were scattered all around the marketplace.
> In Afghanistan last month, another terrorist blew himself up near a crowd gathered for a ceremony to open a hospital emergency ward. A few days later, a Sunni Muslim blew herself up and forty others at a college in Baghdad.

---

1. Cook, *The Cross of Christ: Sufficient to Save*, back cover.

22—Donating Blood to an Enemy

In all three cases, Muslims blew up Muslims. The response of Europe and the Muslim world to the stories of death? Outrage? No. Silence. Did the Western press condemn them? No.

Last week, another story was told on NBC News—this time, a riveting story of life. NBC has been running a gripping series on the emergency military triage facilities in Iraq. Last Thursday, NBC showed wounded Iraqi insurgents being brought to Camp Speicher near Tikrit. Two of them had been caught placing an explosive device on a nearby road, intending to kill Americans, when a U.S. helicopter opened fire on them.

The U.S. medical team moved heaven and earth to save their lives. One insurgent, however, was not going to survive unless he got thirty pints of blood. But the base was low on blood. The call went out for volunteer donors; minutes later, dozens of G.I.s had lined up.

At the head of the line was a battle-hardened soldier named Brian Suam. Asked if it mattered that his blood was going to an insurgent, he smiled and said, no—"A human life is a human life."

I have never seen a more dramatic example of worldviews in contrast, nor have I been prouder of an American G.I. On one hand, we have the horrors of a civilization that values death—even the death of its own children, if by killing them they can hurt the infidels. On the other side, we have a story that makes us realize just how deeply embedded within American life is our Judeo-Christian heritage. This heritage teaches [us] that human life is sacred—even the life of an enemy who falls into our hands.[2]

And, I would add, human life is sacred because we are created in the image of God and because we are potentially redeemed through the blood of God's Son. Remember St. Paul's words in Romans 5:6–10? Here they are:

> For while we were still helpless, at the right time Christ died for the ungodly. For one will hardly die for a righteous man; though perhaps for the good man someone would dare even to die. But God demonstrates His own love toward us, in that while we were yet sinners, Christ died for us. Much more then, having now been justified *by His blood*, we shall be saved from the wrath of God through Him. For if while we were *enemies* we were reconciled to God through the death of His Son, much more, having been reconciled, we shall be saved by His life (italics mine).

---

2. Colson, "Why U.S. Soldiers Donate Blood to Injured Terrorists," *Breakpoint*, March 6, 2007, brackets mine.

In other words, we were God's enemies when His Son gave His blood for us. And He didn't give just a pint or two. He allowed sinful men to torture Him, crucify Him, and plunge a spear into His pericardium, thereby draining out water and blood—most of what was left of His already badly depleted supply. He donated virtually all of His precious blood (probably about ten pints) to make the final and complete atonement for your sins and mine.

We should—and will—spend eternity worshiping and thanking Him for that. We will see Him in heaven as "a Lamb standing, as if slain" (Rev 5:6), and we will sing "a new song, saying, 'Worthy are You to take the book and to break its seals; for You were slain, and purchased for God *with Your blood* men from every tribe and tongue and people and nation'" (Rev 5:9, italics mine). Do you see yourself in that joy-filled throng?

Day 23

THE UNTHINKABLE GOD

*The incarnation is a kind of vast joke whereby
the Creator of the ends of the earth comes among
us in diapers . . . Until we too have taken the idea
of the God-man seriously enough to be scandalized by it,
we have not taken it as seriously as it demands to be taken.*

—FREDERICK BUECHNER[1]

THE WHOLE CLAIM OF Christianity—that Jesus of Nazareth was God—strains the limits of our imagination, if not our credulity. Think about it: Jesus claimed to be God in the flesh. And His representatives perpetuated His claim. They *believed* it. But imagine actually meeting someone who claimed to be God!

The Jews were rightly proud of their monotheism. There was but one true God. But they had so defined His being that it left no room for the staggering concept of "Trinity." It is hardly surprising that they misunderstood Jesus, who was not claiming to be another "god" but was, rather, pointing to His essential unity with the one true God—a claim that was even more overwhelming. He claimed to be indistinguishable from God the Father in respect to His will and His work. You have to understand that to the average first-century Jew, and to the Jewish religious leaders in particular, this

---

1. Buechner, *The Faces of Jesus: A Life Story*, page unknown by me.

was unthinkable. Actually, everything about Him was unthinkable! And, if He really was God, then we'd have to say He was—and is—the *unthinkable* God! How so?

Well, first of all, His *birth* was unthinkable. I mean, according to Dr. Luke, He was born of a *virgin*. That He was "born" at all was unthinkable. How could the eternal God be *born*—let alone as a human being? That He was born of a virgin was *really* unthinkable! The whole concept of God supernaturally reduced to an embryo in a Jewish peasant woman's womb was, on the surface, absurd. But, to the students of the Hebrew Scriptures, it shouldn't really have been such a surprise, for their prophets had indicated that it would be this way. They had predicted that the Messiah would indeed be born into the human race, be born of a virgin, and be called Emmanuel—God with us. Still . . . that God would be here on this planet with us . . . as one of us . . . was unthinkable!

Second, His *life* was unthinkable. I mean, He never sinned! He never did anything wrong! He never indulged an evil thought in His mind, never coveted or lusted in His heart, and never hurt anyone except in the interest of truth and the ultimate good of all concerned. He never succumbed to the raw or subtle temptations of the devil, never caved in to the pressure from His peers, never abandoned His mission in order to please His skeptical siblings, never catered to the corrupt religious establishment, and never challenged the God-ordained order of the existing political system.

He demonstrated an unprecedented degree of compassion. He cared deeply about hurting people, and He spent time with them in crowds, in small groups, and in very personal encounters. He went about doing good, healing all who were oppressed by the devil. He healed every kind of sickness, disease, handicap, and infirmity. He ordered demons to leave the people they had afflicted. On occasion, He even raised people from the dead.

Simon Peter, after spending over three years with Him, said that He committed no sin, nor was any deceit found in His mouth. Other than their unexamined charge of blasphemy—because He made Himself out to be equal with God, the Jewish religious leaders failed to establish that He'd committed one sin. Pilate, the Roman governor who ultimately, but reluctantly, sentenced Him to death, said three times, "I find no guilt in Him." Human experience, ever since the fall of Adam and Eve in the Garden of Eden, had prepared no one to expect anything resembling such a life!

Now students of the Hebrew Scriptures should have expected such a person, for Isaiah had predicted that the Suffering Servant would do no

23—The Unthinkable God

violence nor would there be any deceit in His mouth. And he had predicted that He would bring good news to the afflicted, bind up the brokenhearted, and proclaim liberty to captives and freedom to prisoners. But still . . . such a life was simply unthinkable!

Third, Jesus' *arrest* was unthinkable. Why would anyone need to arrest someone who lived a perfect life? Why should someone who committed no crime be seized and bound by the authorities? Why should they come with lanterns, torches, swords, and clubs to arrest an unarmed, non-violent man? Why should they come at night to a secluded garden to arrest a man who carried on a very public ministry, most of it in broad daylight? And why should their intended "suspect" need to be identified with a kiss on the cheek by a formerly trusted associate?

Even more to the point, why did Jesus even allow this to happen? Why didn't He allow His followers to put up a fight? Why did He rebuke Peter when he, at least, tried? Why did He restore the ear to the slave of the high priest after Peter had sliced it off with his sword? Why, when He Himself indicated that He could have called some 72,000 angels to His defense with an appeal to His Father, did He not do so? His arrest, I say again, was unthinkable!

Then, fourth, Jesus' *trials* were unthinkable. How do you *try* God?! Who has the right to sit in judgment on the God of the universe who has visited the creatures of His creation—let alone to do it with false witnesses who don't even agree with each other and to do it without ever evaluating or examining the possible truthfulness of the defendant's claims?!

On one of many such occasions, I sat in a courtroom at the York County Judicial Center in York, Pennsylvania, and observed a judge's sentencing of at least five individuals, only one of whom I knew. Each was guilty of various crimes and had pled guilty to those crimes. Each was represented by an attorney or was told to return with an attorney at his or her next appearance in court. Each was treated with dignity and respect and called "Mr." or "Miss" or "Ms." Each was clearly apprised of his or her rights—including the right to withdraw a guilty plea and the right to appeal to a higher court. Each was allowed to have family members and friends present in the room during the proceedings. Each was repeatedly asked, "Do you understand?"

None of these statements could be made about Jesus' trials—in spite of the fact that both the Jews and the Romans prided themselves on judicial systems that were fair and impartial. In the courtroom where I sat as a spectator, no one hit the defendants. No sheriff's deputies slapped them, punched them, jammed a crown made out of two-inch-long thorns into their scalps, stripped them, whipped their naked backs with pellet-studded leather straps, mocked them, spat on them, or ridiculed them. But that's exactly what the attending police officers did to Jesus.

In that York County courtroom I saw patience, fairness, courtesy, kindness, justice, and mercy. In Jesus' trials, any impartial observer saw none of those commodities. In fact, such an observer saw the greatest miscarriage of justice in human history! A totally innocent man—in fact, the God-Man—was sentenced to death by crucifixion, a form of capital punishment reserved for common criminals and enemies of the state. His trials were absolutely unthinkable!

And, fifth, His *death* was unthinkable. For one thing, how can God die? Of course, God had taken on a human body, but, still, it was totally unthinkable. I mean, the holy God—the Second Person of the triune Godhead—was at the mercy of grossly sinful men! His hands and feet were nailed to those rough crossbeams, and then He was lifted up to hang there in utter agony until He expired. Today's state executions—usually of deserving, guilty felons—are typically, at least in America, as humane as they can be. They're carried out by lethal injection or by electrocution and are usually over in a matter of seconds.[2]

But this one involved hours of torture—unimaginable pain, sweat, blood, gradual asphyxiation, cramped muscles, and attacks—no doubt—of flying insects with no way to brush them off. This one involved a broken heart, with blood leaking into the pericardium; this one included the puncture, then, of the pericardium with the spear of a Roman soldier. Not only was it true that He came to His own, and His own received Him not, it was also true that He was despised, disrespected, forsaken, and rejected by them. He was literally thrown out, discarded like so much garbage, by the people He came to love, to help, and to save.

But, amazingly, *by* His death—that of the innocent for the guilty, the just for the unjust—He reconciled us to God and made it possible for God to forgive us of our sins. And *in* His death, He—the good shepherd—became the sacrificial lamb, the Lamb of God who by His atoning death took

---

2. I'm aware that in recent times the method of lethal injection has come under intense scrutiny because of the unusually prolonged death of at least two death-row inmates, thanks to the use of experimental combinations of drugs when pharmaceutical companies refused to provide those previously used.

23 — The Unthinkable God

away the sins of the world. Who but God would have conceived such a plan? His death, I say, was unthinkable.

And, finally, Jesus' *burial* was unthinkable. In the light of who He really was, it was unimaginable that He would be buried in a borrowed tomb, that He would be mourned by so few, and that He would be sealed in a cave with no eulogy or funeral service of any sort. But, more to the point, His burial was unprecedented because He wasn't going to stay dead! Though entombed for about thirty-six hours, His body would not begin to decompose.

You see, He was going to rise from the dead, never to die again! As Peter pointed out in his spontaneous sermon on the Day of Pentecost, "it was impossible for Him to be held in death's power." God would not abandon His soul to Hades, nor allow His Holy One to undergo decay. Jesus' bruised, battered, bloodied, and mutilated body was sown a perishable body, but it was raised an imperishable body. I'm sure you'll agree: His burial was unthinkable!

The first-century Jewish religious leaders—and the mob they incited to such an irrational frenzy—wanted to kill Jesus and be done with the unthinkable God. As Nick Mercer puts it, "Emmanuel, God with us, is far too uncomfortable when we want to be left to our own devices."[3] He's too much of a disturbing presence. He's a disrupter of the status quo. He can't be tamed. He's not only the Lamb of God, He's the Lion of Judah! It's unthinkable, but this unthinkable God loves *me* . . . and *you*!

---

3. Mercer, *Encounter with God*, Jan/Feb/Mar, 1999, 82.

Day 24

The Pitfall of the Once-for-All Sacrifice

> *Cheap grace is the preaching of forgiveness*
> *without requiring repentance,*
> *baptism without church discipline,*
> *Communion without confession,*
> *absolution without personal confession.*
> *Cheap grace is grace without discipleship,*
> *grace without the cross,*
> *grace without Jesus Christ,*
> *living and incarnate.*
>
> —Dietrich Bonhoeffer[1]

I invite you to look closely at the first ten verses of the tenth chapter of the Letter to the Hebrews:

> For the Law, since it has only a shadow of the good things to come and not the very form of things, can never, by the same sacrifices which they offer continually year by year, make perfect those who draw near. Otherwise, would they not have ceased to be offered,

---

1. Bonhoeffer, *The Cost of Discipleship*, 36.

24—The Pitfall of the Once-for-All Sacrifice

because the worshipers, having once been cleansed, would no longer have had consciousness of sins? But in those sacrifices there is a reminder of sins year by year. For it is impossible for the blood of bulls and goats to take away sins.

Therefore, when He comes into the world, He says, "SACRIFICE AND OFFERING YOU HAVE NOT DESIRED, BUT A BODY YOU HAVE PREPARED FOR ME; IN WHOLE BURNT OFFERINGS AND SACRIFICES FOR SIN YOU HAVE TAKEN NO PLEASURE. THEN I SAID, 'BEHOLD, I HAVE COME (IN THE SCROLL OF THE BOOK IT IS WRITTEN OF ME) TO DO YOUR WILL, O GOD.'"

After saying above, "SACRIFICES AND OFFERINGS AND WHOLE BURNT OFFERINGS AND SACRIFICES FOR SIN YOU HAVE NOT DESIRED, NOR HAVE YOU TAKEN PLEASURE IN THEM" (which are offered according to the Law), then He said, "BEHOLD, I HAVE COME TO DO YOUR WILL." He takes away the first in order to establish the second. By this will we have been sanctified through the offering of the body of Jesus Christ *once for all* (Heb 10:1–10, italics mine).[2]

Now contemplate this commentary on the passage by John Fieldsend of England:

For those who take the inspiration of the whole of Scripture seriously, this passage succinctly sums up the problem we have with this letter. How can God have established the whole Law/tabernacle/sacrificial system in such detail in Israel's wilderness wanderings and then say that he neither desired them nor was pleased with them (Ps 40:6–8)? To resolve this we will look at their fulfillment in the death of Jesus.

God the Father did not eagerly desire the death of his Son; he did not spare his own Son (Rom 8:32), and this must have caused him grief beyond anything we can imagine. Similarly, Jesus did not wish to die; he earnestly prayed that, if possible, there might be some other way (Matt 26:39, 42). The whole tabernacle/temple system was instigated by God to show his holiness and the awfulness of sin. It was not for God's benefit but to give the people of Israel, and through them all people, an understanding of the one and only way that sin could be atoned for. There are two reasons why the Old Testament sacrifices had to be repeated, because they did not actually achieve what they were demonstrating, and second, because the people continued to sin. Each individual and

---

2. The words in capital letters, in the policy of the *NASB*, reflect quotations from the Old Testament—in this case, Psalm 40:6–8.

> each generation had to be constantly reminded of their need of atonement.
>
> All this underlines for us the wonder of the scale and scope of the "once for all" sacrifice Jesus made on our account (v. 10). But it also highlights *a pitfall that we need to watch*. Because we do not have the symbolic aid of daily repeated sacrifices, we can all too easily become blasé about the costliness of our atonement, and therefore become all too casual about sin in our own lives. We need to apply the psalmist's words regarding Jesus to ourselves. "I have come to do your will" (Ps 40:8).[3]

We know Jesus' agonizing and awesome atonement was *once for all*. We know it never can be, never should be, never needs to be, and never will be repeated. But let's never allow its impact on our worship and our lifestyle to be lost—lost in ancient history or lost to our present consciousness. Paul never wanted it to be lost to him. In fact, as we've already seen, he exclaimed, "But may it never be that I would boast, except in the cross of our Lord Jesus Christ, through which the world has been crucified to me, and I to the world" (Gal 6:14). As we saw on Day 20, He said, "I die daily" (1 Cor 15:31).

He embraced what happened on that cross as the all-sufficient *atonement* for all his sins—past, present, and future, the all-sufficient *antidote* to the power of temptation and sin in the present, and the all-sufficient *alienation* from the very presence of sin in the future. There's no way he ever became blasé about the atonement or casual about any temptation toward or emergence of sin in his life. Nor should we! Let's face it: when the chips are down,

> Cultural Christianity simply won't survive. Comfortable Christianity won't cut it. Convenient Christianity won't pass the test. Casual Christ-following won't withstand the heat. Superficial saints won't measure up. Only authentic ones will. What about you? What about me?[4]

There *are* such theological distortions as "greasy grace" and "sloppy agápē," and we should not succumb to either of those! We need to take seriously—very seriously—our practical response to the unfathomably costly, once-for-all sacrifice of our crucified Lord!

---

3. Fieldsend, *Encounter with God*, Jul/Aug/Sep 2006, 22, italics mine.
4. Oldfield, *Gut-Level Godliness: Authentic Shepherding in a Superficial Age*, 7.

Day 25

Four Crosses

The dying thief rejoiced to see that fountain in his day;
and there may I, though vile as he, wash all my sins away . . .
—WILLIAM COWPER[1]

CAPITAL PUNISHMENT IN THE days of the Roman Empire for convicted criminals who were not Roman citizens was accomplished, as you know, not by electrocution, lethal injection, or poisonous gas, nor even by the guillotine or the gallows, but by the torturous, barbaric, and inhumane method called *crucifixion*. But after the criminal was condemned and sentenced to death and before he was actually affixed by nails through his wrists and feet to the crude wooden crossbeams and suspended until death on the uplifted cross, he had to carry his own cross (or at least its transverse beam) from the scene of his sentencing to the scene of his execution.

On the morning following the previous evening's Passover meal Jesus celebrated with His disciples, three men picked up their crosses and began to carry them to a place called in Hebrew and Aramaic *Golgotha* and in Latin *Calvarius* or *Calvary*—meaning, "The Skull." Dr. Luke says in the historical Gospel named after him that, "When they led Him [Jesus] away, they seized a man, Simon of Cyrene, coming in from the country,

---

1. Cowper, "There Is a Fountain Filled with Blood," Verse 2, 1772 (public domain).

and placed on *him* the cross to carry behind Jesus" (Luke 23:26, brackets and italics mine). Additionally, Luke reports, "Two others also, who were criminals, were being led away to be put to death with Him" (Luke 23:32). So, I say again, *three* men took up their crosses, and though one, due to His unusually weakened condition, relinquished His cross for part of the journey to a *fourth* party, the same three men were nailed to their crosses and died on those crosses that afternoon.

What happened on each of those crosses? What was the significance of each of the deaths that took place there? Well, as Luke explains,

> When they came to the place called The Skull, there they crucified Him and the criminals, one on the right and the other on the left . . . One of the criminals who were hanged there was hurling abuse at Him, saying, "Are You not the Christ? Save Yourself and us!" But the *other* answered, and rebuking him said, "Do you not even fear God, since you are under the same sentence of condemnation? And we indeed are suffering justly, for we are receiving what we deserve for our deeds; but this man has done nothing wrong" (Luke 23:33, 39–41, italics mine).

The *first criminal*—representative, unfortunately, of the majority of the human race—refused to repent and believe. He was sorry he'd been caught, but not particularly sorry he'd sinned. His main concern was getting out of the jam he was in, but since that was quite obviously impossible, he was bitter and angry—at the soldiers, at the governor, at the system, maybe at fellow criminals who got away, perhaps at a "snitch" who had turned him in to the state, probably at the crowd that stood there gaping at him, and at God—at Jesus, who hung tormented and dying on the cross next to him. He was one of those people who blame everyone else for their problems. Too cynical even to note what was happening on the cross next to him and who it was who hung there, he missed the opportunity of a lifetime. In essence, he cursed God and died. Sin and crime paid off in his life, all right. "The wages of sin is death" (Rom. 6:23a)—spiritual, physical, and eternal death.

The *second criminal*—representative, unfortunately, of only a minority of the human race—did repent and believe. He recognized his sinful self, he realized the justness of his sentence of death, he acknowledged that he deserved to die for his sins and crimes, and thus he repented. He took careful note of what was happening on the cross next to Him and who it was who hung there. He realized Jesus' innocence, maybe even His sinlessness. He recognized His kingship, His Messiahship, maybe even His deity. He

25—Four Crosses

knew He needed Him—desperately—not to get off the cross and out of his present predicament, but to be ready for eternity and the future Messianic kingdom. So, he cried out, "Jesus, *remember me* when You come in Your kingdom!" (Luke 23:42, italics mine). And Jesus responded to his repentance and faith by saying, "Truly I say to you, today you shall be with Me in Paradise" (Luke 23:43). The payment for sin is death, all right, "but the free gift of God is eternal life through Jesus Christ our Lord" (Rom 6:23b).

The *third Person* dying on a cross on Golgotha that day was Jesus of Nazareth. But He was not dying for any crimes or sins of His own. He had never committed any. He "committed no sin, nor was any deceit found in His mouth; and while being reviled, He did not revile in return; while suffering, He uttered no threats, but kept entrusting Himself to Him who judges righteously" (1 Pet 2:22-23). So why was He there? He died, "the just for the unjust, so that He might bring us to God" (1 Pet 3:18). "He Himself bore our sins in His body on the cross, that we might die to sin and live to righteousness" (1 Pet 2:24). Jesus died for the other two men, for the two criminals hanging on His right and left. Please understand, though: His death was to no avail for the first one, but it made all the difference in the world to the second.

But I also see a *fourth cross* on Calvary's hill. Many of us reading this today probably claim to be followers of Jesus. What, then, did He have to say to us about what it means to follow Him? He said, "If anyone wishes to come after Me, he must deny himself, and *take up his cross* and follow Me. For whoever wishes to save his life will lose it; but whoever loses his life for My sake will find it. For what will it profit a man if he gains the whole world and forfeits his soul? Or what will a man give in exchange for his soul?" (Matt 16:24-26, italics mine) He also said, "Truly, truly, I say to you, unless a grain of wheat falls into the earth and dies, it remains alone; but if it dies, it bears much fruit. He who loves his life loses it, and he who hates his life in this world will keep it to life eternal" (John 12:24-25). Not only that, but Paul said, "I have been crucified with Christ . . ." (Gal 2:20).

The point is that you and I need to take up *our* cross and be willing, yes, to die for our Lord and for righteousness, as hundreds or even thousands of our brothers and sisters in Him will do this year around the world. But we also need to begin *now* to die to our self, our sin, our personal agenda, our previous master, and the world's value system and live a life characterized by His righteousness. We need to subordinate our will to the will of God, as Jesus did in Gethsemane. We need, as many are saying today, to submit willingly to "cruciform"—to live a cross-shaped life.

As my beloved mentor, Vernon Grounds, related in a book he wrote years ago,

> Mildred Cable grew up in Great Britain, a deeply dedicated, single-minded disciple, headed for a ministry to China. But she met a fellow-disciple and fell in love with him. He more than returned her love and naturally wanted to marry her. Mildred, though, was convinced God was leading her to China. The man she loved, however, was equally convinced God wanted him to remain in England to serve there as a pastor. They prayed, talked, and wept together, but neither could sense the freedom to abandon what seemed to be the definite will of God. One night they kissed each other good-bye and with heartbreak ended their relationship. Mildred's biographer concludes that chapter in her life with one terse sentence: "That night she died." Oh, she went on living long years afterward, but that night she died to her own desires, her own hopes, her own humanly legitimate dreams. She died to her *own* will [in order] to carry out the will of God. She went to China, where God gave her the joy and blessing of an extraordinarily fruitful ministry."[2]

Remember: she died . . . and thus she bore much fruit.

So, Jesus said if we wanted to be His disciple, we'd have to take up *our* cross and die. Now why would we do that? Out of love for Him who loved us and gave Himself up on *His* cross for us! Out of a desire to please Him who pleased not Himself but died that agonizing death for our eternal benefit!

Do you love Him today?? Then die. And begin to live!

---

2. Grounds, *YBH—Yes, But How?—Getting Serious About Your Faith*, page unknown by me, italics and brackets mine.

Day 26

Don't Forget Gethsemane— the Agony of Decision!

Gethsemane is where He died; the cross is only the evidence.
—Leonard Ravenhill[1]

As you know, when Jesus instituted what we have come to call "The Lord's Supper," He said, "This do in remembrance of Me" (Luke 22:19). In other words, Jesus said to His first-century disciples and indirectly to His twenty-first century disciples, just what our mothers, fathers, teachers, friends, and spouses have often had occasion to say to us: "Don't forget!" But, in essence, He added: "And just to be sure you don't forget, I want you regularly—until I come back—to re-enact what we're doing here tonight at this, My last supper with you. Every time you do this, every time you observe this supper again, you'll find it that much easier to remember Me."

I ask you: Does a ritual, a ceremony like this, really help? I answer with another question: How about the Passover—which is exactly what Jesus and His disciples had originally met that night to observe? The Jews had faithfully observed the Passover Feast for 1,470 years, ever since the Exodus in 1441 BC! And now the church of Jesus Christ has been observing The

---

1. Ravenhill, "Are We Willing to Drink His Cup?"

Prizing His Passion

Lord's Supper for nearly 2,000 years, ever since the original Last Supper in AD 30![2]

At any rate, surely it wasn't likely that Jesus' disciples were going to forget Him! Yet what, specifically, do you suppose He was urging them not to forget? I believe the Lord Jesus urged them that night, in essence, not to forget *four places* and the *agonies* associated with them, all of which were yet future when He spoke.

I believe He was saying, first of all, "Don't forget *Gethsemane*! Don't forget *the agony of decision*!" Gethsemane, which means "oil press," was an olive yard, a garden east of Jerusalem beyond the brook Kidron at the foot of the Mount of Olives. It was the place where Jesus wrestled with the issues and made His final decision to go ahead with His mission on earth and to fulfill it. Here's what happened there:

> Then Jesus came with them to a place called *Gethsemane*, and said to His disciples, "Sit here while I go over there and pray." And He took with Him Peter and the two sons of Zebedee [James and John], and began to be grieved and distressed. Then He said to them, "My soul is deeply grieved, to the point of death; remain here and keep watch with Me."
>
> And He went a little beyond them, and fell on His face and prayed, saying, "My Father, if it is possible, let this cup pass from Me; yet not as I will, but as You will." And He came to the disciples and found them sleeping, and said to Peter, "So, you men could not keep watch with Me for one hour? Keep watching and praying that you may not enter into temptation; the spirit is willing, but the flesh is weak."
>
> He went away again a second time and prayed, saying, "My Father, if this cannot pass away unless I drink it, Your will be done." Again He came and found them sleeping, for their eyes were heavy. And He left them again, and went away and prayed a third time, saying the same thing once more. Then He came to the disciples and said to them, "Are you still sleeping and resting? Behold, the hour is at hand and the Son of Man is being betrayed into the hands of sinners. Get up, let us be going; behold, the one who betrays Me is at hand!" (Matt 26:36–46, italics and brackets mine)

In the parallel account in Luke's Gospel, the author—a physician, you will recall—says, "And being in *agony* He was praying very fervently; and His sweat became like drops of blood, falling down to the ground" (Luke 22:44,

---

2. I'm assuming, but not dogmatically, the accuracy of the A.D. 30 date. See relevant footnote on Day 9.

26—Don't Forget Gethsemane—the Agony of Decision!

italics mine). It is often difficult, lonely, and even heart-wrenching to decide to do the will of God in a given matter, but "as a result of the *anguish* of [our] soul," as in the case of Jesus, we will one day, in a less profound sense, "see it" [see victory, see fruitfulness] "and be satisfied" (Isa 53:11, italics and brackets mine). Like Him, though, we need first to say to God, "Not as I will, but as You will."

As we saw in yesterday's commentary, to terminate a relationship that's outside the will of God and/or that is hindering your priority relationship to Him, especially when much emotional attachment has built up in the relationship, is a difficult, even agonizing, thing. To stop indulging a sinful habit or addiction, especially when your flesh cries out in pain and protest at the very thought of not being pampered and fed, is a difficult, even agonizing, thing. To heed the call of God to leave friends, loved ones, and familiar surroundings to go hundreds of miles away to prepare for His service or to go thousands of miles away to serve Him as a missionary is a difficult, even agonizing, thing.

To begin following Jesus and to alter a life-style it's taken months or years to establish—whether it's oriented to the drug culture, the jet set, the streets, the glitzy and seemingly glamorous world of entertainment, or the nice, non-offensive, middle-class, middle-of-the-road culture of rural areas or suburbia—is not easy. It's a difficult, even agonizing, thing. St. Peter rightly urged, "Since Christ has suffered in the flesh, arm yourselves also with the same purpose, because he who has suffered in the flesh has ceased from sin, so as to live the rest of the time in the flesh no longer for the lusts of men, but for the will of God" (1 Pet 4:1–2).

Jesus appealed intensely to His Father—and, no doubt, wrestled mightily with Satan—in that garden on that fateful night. Unlike us, He was born with no bent toward evil and, unlike us, did not, therefore, have to deal with sinful "flesh" that wanted to be satisfied illegitimately. But He still had to wrestle with His own physical flesh—His totally vulnerable, physical being. To drink the impending cup of suffering would be to experience a depth of suffering in the spiritual realm that was unprecedented—and unduplicated—in the history of the human race. He could have refused, because the price would simply be too great. He could have turned back, because the indescribable pain that awaited Him appeared intolerable. Who could have faulted Him, had He chosen to take the easy road and left us to fend for ourselves?

But He chose to go the way of the cross and provide for our salvation. What would have become of us, if He hadn't? The only hope for all of us would have died in the garden if He had not chosen to "drink the cup." Whatever you do, don't forget Gethsemane! Don't forget the agony of decision!

Day 27

Don't Forget Gabbatha—
the Agony of Desecration!

*From a legal point of view this trial represented
the greatest miscarriage of justice and the greatest hoax
that has ever been perpetrated against any person in all history.
It was fraudulent from start to finish,
illegal at almost every point and on every possible count.
It was anything but a trial in which justice was in view
in the desire of those conducting it.*

—Roy Cogdill[1]

When Jesus said, to His disciples at The Last Supper, "Do this in remembrance of Me," I believe He was also saying, "Don't forget *Gabbatha*! Don't forget *the agony of desecration*!" Gabbatha, which means "pavement," was an open space covered with a mosaic of colored stones at the front of the governor's Praetorium in Jerusalem. It was the place where Pontius Pilate sat to judge Jesus, the place where Jesus experienced the desecration of His civil rights, His human dignity, His physical body, and His divine majesty. Here's what happened there:

1. Cogdill, "The Trial of Jesus," *Truth Magazine,* Guardian of Truth XXXI:20, October 15, 1987, 615.

> Pilate then took Jesus and scourged Him. And the soldiers twisted together a crown of thorns and put it on His head, and put a purple robe on Him; and they began to come up to Him and say, "Hail, King of the Jews!" and to give Him slaps in the face.
>
> Pilate came out again and said to them [the Jewish religious leaders and the gathered crowd], "Behold, I am bringing Him out to you so that you may know that I find no guilt in Him." Jesus then came out, wearing the crown of thorns and the purple robe. Pilate said to them, "Behold, the Man!"
>
> So when the chief priests and the officers saw Him, they cried out saying, "Crucify, crucify!" Pilate said to them, "Take Him yourselves and crucify Him, for I find no guilt in Him." The Jews answered him, "We have a law, and by that law He ought to die because He made Himself out to be the Son of God."
>
> Therefore when Pilate heard this statement, he was even more afraid; and he entered into the Praetorium again and said to Jesus, "Where are You from?" But Jesus gave him no answer. So Pilate said to Him, "You do not speak to me? Do You not know that I have authority to release You, and I have authority to crucify You?" Jesus answered, "You would have no authority over Me, unless it had been given you from above; for this reason he who delivered Me to you has the greater sin."
>
> As a result of this Pilate made efforts to release Him, but the Jews cried out saying, "If you release this Man, you are no friend of Caesar; everyone who makes himself out to be a king opposes Caesar." Therefore when Pilate heard these words, he brought Jesus out, and sat down on the judgment seat at a place called The Pavement, but in Hebrew, *Gabbatha*.
>
> Now it was the day of preparation for the Passover; it was about the sixth hour [noon]. And he said to the Jews, "Behold, your King!" So they cried out, "Away with Him, away with Him, crucify Him!" Pilate said to them, "Shall I crucify your King?" The chief priests answered, "We have no king but Caesar." So he then handed Him over to them to be crucified (John 19:1–16, italics and brackets mine).

Jesus—the sinless, blameless, perfect Son of God—was punched, slapped, crowned with thorns, de-bearded, spat upon, cursed, taunted, mocked, ridiculed, whipped, falsely accused, unfairly tried, unjustly sentenced, despised, and rejected by men. The violations of His civil rights under both Jewish law and Roman law were multiple and egregious:

27—Don't Forget Gabbatha—the Agony of Desecration!

- Witnesses, not judges, should initiate trials; yet the High Priest, the ex-High Priest, and the members of the Sanhedrin (the Jewish Council) conspired to conduct this one.
- Judges should not go out looking for witnesses, but that's exactly what they did.
- When none were found, they shouldn't have proceeded with the trial; instead they produced *false* witnesses, whose testimonies didn't even agree with one another.
- They should never have granted credence to those "witnesses," let alone used their testimonies; ordinarily, Jewish law bent over backwards to protect the accused from false condemnation.
- The truthfulness of Jesus' claim to be God was never tested; once the claim itself was established, He was condemned in His Jewish trial.
- While Jewish law forbade attempts to make an accused person incriminate himself, the judges used Jesus' testimony against Himself.
- Contrary to the Mishna, which stipulated that a capital trial must be started only in the daytime and finished during daytime on the same day if there is an acquittal or on the second day if there is a sentence of condemnation, Jesus' trial was held during the night.
- The trial should not have been held on the eve of Passover, a sacrosanct time; but it was.
- According to Jewish law, a man could not be sentenced on the same day his trial was held, but Jesus was tried and sentenced on the same day.
- Jesus was struck on the face, spat upon, and beaten with fists, all violations of His civil rights.
- The charges the Jewish leaders presented to Pontius Pilate, the roman procurator—that Jesus was perverting the nation, forbidding Jewish citizens to give tribute (taxes) to Caesar, and claiming to be a (temporal) king—were utterly false.
- Pilate found Jesus innocent, yet—upon discovering He was a Galilean—passed Him off to Herod Antipas, the tetrarch of Galilee, who happened to be in Jerusalem at the time.
- After Herod, before whom Jesus refused to "perform," sent Him back to Pilate, Pilate again declared Him innocent and proposed to have

Him scourged and released; but it was illegal to scourge an innocent man, and, besides that, He, having been declared innocent, should have been acquitted.

As Jesus said to His followers,

> "If the world hates you, you know that it has hated Me before it hated you. If you were of the world, the world would love its own; but because you are not of the world, but I chose you out of the world, because of this the world hates you. Remember the word that I said to you, 'A slave is not greater than his master.' If they persecuted Me, they will also persecute you; if they kept My word, they will keep yours also. But all these things they will do to you for My name's sake, because they do not know the One who sent Me" (John 15:18–21).

It's often difficult, even agonizing, to be mocked in the public-school or college or university classroom for your objection to the Darwinian theory of evolution and your stand for the biblical doctrine of creation. It's often difficult, even agonizing, to be ridiculed in the locker room for your unwillingness to discuss members of the opposite sex as pieces of meat and objects of lust rather than persons of dignity and objects of honor and respect. It's often difficult, even agonizing, to be accused in the factory or office of bigotry, narrow-mindedness, and wrong motives for your attempts to share the gospel with your fellow-workers. It's often difficult, even agonizing, to be maligned in the neighborhood for your refusal to get high, get drunk, participate in a burglary, commit an act of violence or vandalism, or join a gang.

It's often difficult, even agonizing, to express—however humbly and gently—your Bible-based views on the sinfulness of homosexuality, bisexuality, transsexuality, heterosexual cohabitation outside of marriage, premarital sex of any variety, and abortion (in the light of the sanctity of human life) and then be called bigoted, homophobic, judgmental, and hopelessly behind the times and accused of trying to impose your religious views on others. It's often difficult, even agonizing, to be rejected by family members and friends and called a religious fanatic or a "Jesus freak" just because, as a sinner, you saw your deep need for the salvation Jesus purchased for you, gladly accepted it, and tried to encourage them to do the same.

But have you read of the desecration of the civil rights of fellow-believers in Communist, Muslim, and Hindu-dominated countries—the trumped-up charges, the torturous interrogations, the traumatizing

27—Don't Forget Gabbatha—The Agony of Desecration!

incarcerations, the inhumane treatment? Some time ago, I read Bob Fu's book called, *God's Double Agent: The True Story of a Chinese Christian's Fight for Freedom*, which was published in 2013. In it he details the grossly unjust, brutal, barbaric treatment of dissidents—especially Christians—by the Chinese government . . . not just in the distant past, but also in the twenty-first century.

But according to Bradford Richardson, writing in June of 2018, Bob Fu has now

> . . . said that the number of people arrested in China for exercising their religious freedom "has reached the highest level since the end of the Cultural Revolution." He cited internal figures showing a nearly fivefold increase in the number of Christians who were persecuted by the government last year [2017]. "For Christians alone, last year we documented persecution against 1,265 churches, with the number of people persecuted over 223,000. And that is just the tip of the iceberg."[2]

If anything, the situation in China has even worsened in 2018 and 2019. And anyone paying attention to the news knows of the atrocities perennially committed against Christians, Jews, and others by ISIS, Boko Haram, Al Qaida, Al Shabaab, Hamas, Hezbollah, and other Islamic militant and terrorist organizations.

If we elect to follow Jesus, we too may well experience the desecration of our civil rights, our human dignity, our physical body, and our precious faith in Him. But, as we saw on Day 19,

> Beloved, do not be surprised at the fiery ordeal among you, which comes upon you for your testing, as though some strange thing were happening to you; but to the degree that you share the sufferings of Christ, keep on rejoicing, so that also at the revelation of His glory you may rejoice with exultation. If you are reviled for the name of Christ, you are blessed, because the Spirit of glory and of God rests on you (1 Pet 4:12–14).

Don't forget Gabbatha! Don't forget the agony of desecration!

---

2. Richardson, *The Washington Times*, June 6, 2018, brackets mine.

Day 28

Don't Forget Golgotha—
The Agony of Death!

See, from his head, his hands, his feet,
sorrow and love flow mingled down.
Did e'er such love and sorrow meet,
or thorns compose so rich a crown?

—Isaac Watts[1]

When Jesus said to His disciples on the eve of His crucifixion, "Do this in remembrance of Me," I believe He was saying, further, "Don't forget *Golgotha*! Don't forget *the agony of death!*" Golgotha, or Calvary, which means "skull," was a hill just outside the walls of ancient Jerusalem. It was the place where Jesus experienced a torturous, agonizing death by crucifixion at the hands of Roman soldiers. Here's what happened there:

> They took Jesus, therefore, and He went out, bearing His own cross, to the place called the Place of a Skull, which is called in Hebrew, *Golgotha*. There they crucified Him, and with Him two other men, one on either side, and Jesus in between.
>
> Pilate also wrote an inscription and put it on the cross. It was written, "JESUS THE NAZARENE, THE KING OF THE JEWS."

---

1. Watts, "When I Survey the Wondrous Cross," Verse 3, 1707 (public domain).

28—Don't Forget Golgotha—The Agony of Death!

> Therefore many of the Jews read this inscription, for the place where Jesus was crucified was near the city; and it was written in Hebrew, Latin and in Greek . . .
>
> Therefore when Jesus had received the sour wine, He said, "It is finished!" And He bowed His head and gave up His spirit (John 19:19–21, 30).

Jesus suffered, bled, and died on Golgotha . . . for you . . . and me. And now He bids *us* come and die. As we've seen more than once, He said, "If any one wishes to come after Me, let him deny himself, and take up his cross, and follow Me. For whoever wishes to save his life shall lose it; but whoever loses his life for My sake shall find it" (Matt 16:24–25). There's a practical, daily death for us as Christians. It's a death to self, sin, Satan, and the world-system.

There may, one day, be a physical, martyr's death for us as well. It's not easy to die either kind of death. It's often difficult, even agonizing, to "consider [ourselves] to be dead to sin, but alive to God in Christ Jesus," and "not [to] let sin reign in [our] mortal bodies that [we] should obey its lusts" (Rom 6:11–12, brackets mine). It's often difficult, even agonizing, to "die daily," as Paul said of his own experience in serving the Lord (1 Cor 15:31), to be for Jesus' sake "put to death all day long," to be "considered as sheep to be slaughtered" (Rom 8:26), to be continually facing the possibility and perhaps, ultimately, the actuality of martyrdom.

I ate breakfast some time ago with an old buddy of mine that I hadn't seen in years. He has spent decades recruiting people who are willing to commit their lives to be Christian missionaries—though usually not by that title—to the Muslim world. And he is such an ambassador himself. He said, "All of us [believers] are interested in seeing the fulfillment of Revelation 5:9 and 7:9, but we tend to forget that the way to get there is through Revelation 6:9."

You see, in the ninth verse of the *fifth* chapter of The Revelation, John hears the four living creatures and the twenty-four elders singing "a new song, saying, 'Worthy are You to take the book and to break its seals; for You were slain and purchased for God with Your blood men from every tribe and tongue and people and nation.'" This is a future a scene in heaven. And in the ninth verse of the *seventh* chapter of The Revelation, John sees "a great multitude which no one could count, from every nation and all tribes and peoples and tongues, standing before the throne and before the Lamb, clothed in white robes, and palm branches were in their hands." This is another future scene in heaven. Both of these scenes indicate clearly that representatives of *every* people-group or *ethnos* on earth (including those of Muslim background) will compose the population of heaven.

But in the ninth verse of the *sixth* chapter of The Revelation, John sees something else: "When the Lamb broke the fifth seal, I saw underneath the altar the souls of those who had been *slain* because of the word of God and because of the testimony which they had maintained" (italics mine). In other words, as our Chinese brothers and sisters in Christ planning to take the gospel "back to Jerusalem"[2] know all too well, it's going to cost dearly to get the gospel to every people and language group. It's going to involve global persecution and widespread martyrdom. That's what my old friend was saying.

So, don't forget Golgotha! Don't forget the agony of death! As William MacDonald has put it, "Anyone who sets out to follow Christ should remember *Gethsemane*, *Gabbatha*, and *Golgotha*. And then he should count the cost. It is either an absolute commitment to Christ, or a sniveling surrender with all that that means of disgrace and degradation."[3] But there's one more place and yet another agony we need to remember. We'll consider it tomorrow.

---

2. The "Back to Jerusalem" movement is a Christian evangelistic thrust initiated in mainland China by Chinese believers for the purpose of sending 100,000 missionaries to all of the Buddhist, Hindu, and Muslim peoples (approximately 5,200 previously unreached people-groups and tribes) who live in the so-called "10/40 window" along the old Silk Road between China and Jerusalem.

3. MacDonald, *True Discipleship*, 57, italics mine.

Day 29

Don't Forget Galilee— the Agony of Declaration!

Am I a soldier of the cross, a foll'wer of the Lamb?
And shall I fear to own His cause or blush to speak His name?
Must I be carried to the skies on flow'ry beds of ease,
While others fought to win the prize and sailed through bloody seas?

—Isaac Watts[1]

When Jesus said to His closest followers on the eve of His crucifixion, "Do this in remembrance of Me," I believe He was saying, finally, "Don't forget *Galilee*! Don't forget *the agony of declaration!*" Galilee, which means "circle," was one of the largest Roman districts of Palestine. It was the primary region of Jesus' ministry. But it was also the place where He said He would meet His disciples for instructions after His crucifixion and resurrection. Here's what He said shortly after He and His disciples concluded their celebration of the Passover by singing a hymn and going out to the Mount of Olives: "You will all fall away because of Me this night, for it is written, 'I WILL STRIKE DOWN THE SHEPHERD, AND THE SHEEP OF THE

---

1. Watts, "Am I a Soldier of the Cross?" Verses 1 & 2, 1724 (public domain).

FLOCK SHALL BE SCATTERED.' But after I have been raised, I will go ahead of you to *Galilee*" (Matt 26:31–32, italics mine).[2]

Now go with me to Easter Sunday morning, and listen to what the angel of the Lord told Mary Magdalene and "the other Mary" at the empty tomb. "The angel said to the women, 'Do not be afraid; for I know that you are looking for Jesus who has been crucified. He is not here, for He has risen, just as He said. Come, see the place where He was lying. Go quickly and tell His disciples that He has risen from the dead; and behold, He is going ahead of you into *Galilee*, there you will see Him; behold, I have told you'" (Matt 28:5–7, italics mine).

Sure enough, that's exactly how it played out just before Jesus' ascension back to the Father:

> But the eleven disciples proceeded to *Galilee*, to the mountain which Jesus had designated. When they saw Him, they worshiped Him; but some were doubtful.
> And Jesus came up and spoke to them, saying, "All authority has been given to Me in heaven and on earth. Go therefore and make disciples of all the nations, baptizing them in the name of the Father and the Son and the Holy Spirit, teaching them to observe all that I commanded you; and lo, I am with you always, even to the end of the age" (Matt 28:16–20, italics mine).

It was no easy task to carry out the "Great Commission" in the first-century Roman world. As we've already seen, in the same breath when the risen Lord told Ananias in Damascus a few years later that Saul of Tarsus was "a chosen instrument of Mine, to bear My name [i.e., declare My gospel] before the Gentiles, and kings and the sons of Israel," He added, "for I will show him how much he must *suffer* for My name's sake" (Acts 9:16, brackets and italics mine). It has never been an easy task to declare or proclaim "repentance for forgiveness of sins . . . in His name to all the nations, beginning from Jerusalem" (Luke 24:47).

In fact, it has been a very difficult, even agonizing thing to proclaim the gospel. Why?

- Because politicians have legislated against it (when it's threatened their power and prestige).

---

2. The words in capital letters indicate a quotation from the Old Testament, in this case Zechariah 13:7.

29 — Don't Forget Galilee — The Agony of Declaration!

- Because merchants have protested against it (when it's threatened their sales and profits).
- Because religious leaders have taught against it (when it's threatened their vested interests).
- Because Satan has hindered it (whenever it's begun to wrest sinners from his grip).
- Because sinners have resisted it (when it's challenged their chosen lifestyle).
- Because insufficient finances have limited it (when believers have failed to prioritize it).
- And because church members have ignored or minimized it (when they've lost their first love).

Yet some have caught the vision and been willing to pay the price. In a newsletter I received many years ago from Bob Bowman, then president of the Far East Broadcasting Company, he quoted an excerpt from a letter sent by a listener in Korea: "I am a man of 48 years, a most brutal and cruel sinner who has been in jail eleven times. But I decided to believe on Jesus Christ while listening to the blind pastor. Rev. Yun, preach on your station . . . I want to present one of my eyes to that blind pastor. Please, will you send me his address so that I may thank him?"

What a demonstration of the love of God in the heart of this new believer, who wanted to give one of his eyes as a gift—to assist a blind pastor in declaring the gospel to others so that they too might be introduced to Christ! God has not specifically asked us to give our eyes; He has, however, asked us to give our bodies—our whole beings—as living sacrifices to Him (Rom 12:1) for Him to use in the declaration of His love and truth.

Do you ever get tired of giving your Faith-Promise offering to your church's missions outreach each month—or your pledge of support to a particular missionary family or organization? In a letter I received some years ago from Ray Eicher, a veteran missionary to India who was raised on the field by missionary parents,[3] he mentioned a dear couple who had been

---

3. My father, Stewart Oldfield, died in the arms of Ray's father, Elmore Eicher, when he suffered a heart attack while kneeling with the retired missionary and another fellow-elder at the front pew of the Alliance Chapel in DeLand, Florida, to pray for a lady who had responded to the invitation at the end of a Sunday morning service in September, 1986. My dad had just concluded his prayer with the words "in Jesus' name. Amen." Ray Eicher, himself, died on August 13, 2016, in Lalitpur, UP, India, after a battle with cancer.

sending the Eicher family a gift each month for forty-seven years! That bespeaks a total of 564 consecutive monthly gifts! Those gifts undoubtedly on many occasions represented a sacrifice; they certainly resulted in less disposable income for personal use.

But the real sacrifices and the demonstrations of real agony associated with the declaration of the gospel come from those who live and labor under intense persecution for their faith and their witness for Christ. They experience social ostracism, limited job opportunities, substandard living conditions, unjustified suspicions, false accusations, demeaning interrogations, brainwashing, physical torture, unjust incarcerations, heart-wrenching separations from their loved ones, and even martyrdom. As I've already indicated, hundreds—probably thousands—of our brothers and sisters in Christ (men, women, and children) will pay the ultimate price this year around the globe.

Although, when it comes to their eternal salvation, Christ-followers can add nothing to the finished work of His Passion without committing blasphemy and embracing false doctrine, they can—according to St. Paul—fill up what is lacking in His afflictions. What could he possibly mean? The context of his startling statement will provide its own answer:

> Now I rejoice in my sufferings for your sake, and in my flesh I do my share on behalf of His body, which is the church, in *filling up what is lacking in Christ's afflictions*. Of this church I was made a minister according to the stewardship from God bestowed on me for your benefit, so that I might fully carry out the preaching of the word of God . . . (Col 1:24–25, italics mine).

Quite simply, as you can see, what's lacking has nothing to do with the price paid by Jesus Christ to purchase our salvation; but it has everything to do with the price paid by His followers to publish it—to proclaim it, to preach it, to spread it throughout the earth. Paul, for example, did nothing to atone for his own sins—nor could he, nor could you or I or anyone else in the history of the human race. But he suffered greatly in his prodigious efforts to proclaim the gospel to everyone in the then-known world. So did everyone else among the early church fathers, and so did huge numbers among its rank-and-file members. So have countless Christ-followers throughout the history of His church to this very moment.

The original agonies of *Gethsemane*, *Gabbatha*, and *Golgotha* were uniquely those of Jesus Christ, our exalted Head. But the original agony of *Galilee* was that of His body—His followers, His church; and that agony

29—Don't Forget Galilee—the Agony of Declaration!

still accompanies the proclamation of the gospel in many places in our own generation. Don't forget Galilee! Don't forget the agony of declaration!

Day 30

THE LIFTING UP OF THE SON OF MAN

Lifted up was He to die; "It is finished!" was His cry;
Now in Heav'n exalted high. Hallelujah! What a Savior!
—PHILIP P. BLISS[1]

I REALIZE THE SAVING grace that has come our way through Jesus Christ of Nazareth is a matter "into which angels long to look" (1 Pet 1:12). And I realize that we in our puny, finite minds cannot possibly plumb the depths of the riches of God's wisdom and knowledge; I realize that His judgments are unsearchable and His ways unfathomable (Rom 11:33). But still, I want you, if not to understand fully, to appreciate more than ever the impact of His offer of salvation. I want you to reflect all over again on the significance of His being *lifted up to die.*

Please understand: contrary to the popular misconception in our generation of Jesus' intended meaning, when He talked about being "lifted up," He was not thinking about being praised or exalted; quite the reverse, He was thinking of being disgraced and humiliated, of being nailed to and then lifted up on a wooden cross as it was raised, then dropped into a hole in the ground, then stabilized . . . with Him hanging on it vertically.

1. Bliss, "Hallelujah! What a Savior!" Verse 4, 1875 (public domain).

30—The Lifting Up of the Son of Man

We are grossly unworthy sinners. Yet Jesus is offering us eternal salvation! But for us to appreciate His offer properly, I'm convinced that we must see three aspects of it, and they appear in the three contexts in John's Gospel where Jesus uses the phraseology "lift up" or "lifted up."

First of all, we must see the *necessity* of His offer. In John 8:38, Jesus said, "When you *lift up* the Son of Man, then you will know that I am He, and I do nothing on My own initiative, but I speak these things as the Father taught Me" (italics mine). What happened when they lifted Him up? Among other things, darkness fell upon all the land from noon until 3:00 P.M. (Matt 27:34), forgiveness was expressed by Jesus (Luke 23:34), the veil in the temple was torn in two from top to bottom (Matt 27:51), and His work of redemption was completed as He cried out, "It is finished!" (John 19:30) Of course, after they had lifted Him up—and taken Him down—and buried Him, He rose from the dead! To say the least, these were all very unusual phenomena, and they validated Jesus' Messianic claims.

Without Him and without His bloody death there is no hope for the sinner. As Jesus Himself declared, "*No one* comes to the Father *but through Me*" (John 14:6, italics mine). As St. Peter announced, "There is salvation in *no one else*" (Acts 4:12, italics mine). As St. Paul explained, "There is one God and *one* mediator also between God and men, the man Christ Jesus" (1 Tim 2:5, italics mine). And as the writer of the Epistle to the Hebrews concluded, "According to the Law one may almost say, all things are cleansed with blood, and *without shedding of blood* there is *no* forgiveness" (Heb 9:22, italics mine). Do you see the *necessity* of Jesus' offer of salvation, of His being "lifted up"?

For us to appreciate the impact of Jesus' offer of salvation, we must also see the *universality* of it. In John 12:32–33, Jesus said, "'And I, if I am *lifted up* from the earth, will draw all men to Myself.' But He was saying this to indicate the kind of death by which He was to die" (italics mine). Once again, I stress that, in spite of some of our worship-chorus lyrics, His words have nothing to do with people exalting Him.

But did you notice? His saving grace will be available to "*all* men"— to Greeks, like those present (according to v. 20) when Jesus spoke these words, as well as to Jews. Yes, His offer is *personal*; it's even for me! As we've already noted, Paul called himself the foremost of sinners, and yet he said of Jesus, "He loved *me* and delivered Himself up for *me*" (Gal 2:20, italics mine). But Paul knew and John said that it's also *universal*: "He Himself is the propitiation for our sins; and not for ours only but also for those of the whole world" (1 John 2:2).

Paul prayed for the Ephesian believers that they might "be able to comprehend with all the saints what is the *breadth* and *length* and *height* and *depth*, and to know the love of Christ which surpasses knowledge, that [they might] be filled up to all the fullness of God" (Eph 3:18–19, italics and brackets mine). Think about it: God's love is *broad* enough to embrace all races and nationalities, *long* enough to last all the way from eternity past through eternity future, *high* enough to lift all believers to the glories of heaven, and *deep* enough to embrace people of all classes and backgrounds—including those characterized by gross sin and depravity. And all of that is most graphically symbolized by the upward and downward sweep of the vertical beam of the cross and the outstretched arms of the One who died on it.

Now, according to verse 34 in John 12, the crowd simply couldn't conceive that Messiah must be *lifted up to die*, because they knew of prophetic passages like Psalm 110:4, Isaiah 9:7, and Daniel 7:14, which use words like "forever," "no end," "everlasting," and "will not pass away" of Messiah and His kingdom. They somehow missed chapters like Psalm 22 and Isaiah 53, which contain vivid descriptions of Messiah's atoning death by crucifixion—to "justify the many." Do you see the *universality* of His offer of salvation, of His being "lifted up"?

For us to appreciate the impact of Jesus' offer of salvation, we must see, too, the *simplicity* of it. In John 3:14–15, Jesus said, "As Moses lifted up the serpent in the wilderness, even so must the Son of Man be *lifted up*; so that whoever believes will in Him have eternal life" (italics mine). Jesus was referring to the account in Numbers 21 during the wilderness wanderings of the Israelites between Egypt and the Promised Land. They had become impatient because of the journey, had complained, and had spoken against God and Moses. So, the Lord became angry with them and sent fiery serpents among the people, leading to the death of many. When the people came to Moses, admitted their sin, and begged him to intercede for them, he did; and the Lord told him to make a fiery serpent of bronze, set it on a standard, and tell the people that whoever simply looked at it would live. Those who did were spared.

Don't you think some probably said, "You're not gonna get me to look at that thing! For one thing, I don't like snakes! For another, it's not scientific! It's disgustingly unsophisticated! It's an insult to my intelligence! It's nothing but superstition! There's got to be something else we're supposed to do! It's too simple; anyone can see that!" In reference to the spilled blood of Jesus as the remedy for sin, Paul said, "For the word of the cross is foolishness to those who are perishing, but to us who are being saved it is the power of God" (1 Cor 1:18). To be saved from our sin and the prospect of eternal damnation, we must look by faith not to a fiery bronze serpent on a pole but to a tortured, bleeding man on a cross. Do you see the *simplicity* of His offer of salvation, of His being "lifted up"?

But could the offer only come about by His being "lifted up" as He was on that awful Roman cross? Yes! It was the *only* plan. There was no "Plan B"! We've already seen that as Jesus wrestled in Gethsemane with what was up ahead and wondered if His Father would allow "this cup" of suffering to pass from Him, the silent answer from the heavens was, "No." We've already seen that Jesus was delivered up by the predetermined plan and foreknowledge of God (Acts 2:23). He was the "lamb unblemished and spotless" who was "foreknown before the foundation of the world" (1 Pet 1:19–20).

For us to appreciate the impact of God's offer of salvation, we must see its necessity, its universality, and its simplicity. Have you seen *your* need? Have you grasped the truth that *you're* included in the plan? Have you personally and pointedly looked to the cross in repentance and faith and been saved from certain eternal death? If not, you *can*—right now!

Day 31

WHATEVER BECAME OF BARABBAS?

> *If it has to choose who is to be crucified,*
> *the crowd will always save Barabbas.*
> —JEAN COCTEAU[1]

JESUS OF NAZARETH HAD been up all day and all night on Thursday. Now it was early Friday morning. For the second time He stood in the city of Jerusalem before Pontius Pilate, the Roman governor or procurator of Palestine. The account appears in all four Gospels, but let's read it in just one:

> Pilate summoned the chief priests and the rulers and the people, and said to them, "You brought this man to me as one who incites the people to rebellion, and behold, having examined Him before you, I have found no guilt in this man regarding the charges which you make against Him. No, nor has Herod, for he sent Him back to us; and behold, nothing deserving death has been done by Him. Therefore I will punish Him and release Him." [Now he was obliged to release to them at the feast one prisoner.][2]
> But they cried out all together, saying, "Away with this man, and release for us Barabbas!" (He was one who had been thrown

---

1. Cocteau, Essay, Le Coq et l'Arlequin, *Le Rappel à L'Ordre*.
2. This verse is in brackets because early manuscripts do not contain it. It was surely added to explain the reason for the release of a prisoner.

31 — Whatever Became of Barabbas?

> into prison for an insurrection made in the city, and for murder.) Pilate, wanting to release Jesus, addressed them again, but they kept on calling out, saying, "Crucify, crucify Him!" And he said to them the third time, "Why, what evil has this man done? I have found in Him no guilt demanding death; therefore I will punish Him and release Him."
>
> But they were insistent, with loud voices asking that He be crucified. And their voices began to prevail. And Pilate pronounced sentence that their demand be granted. And he released the man they were asking for who had been thrown into prison for insurrection and murder, but he delivered Jesus to their will (Luke 23:13–25).

I want to focus today on Barabbas, the man who, instead of Jesus, was released from prison and from Roman custody. What do we know about him? Well, according to Matthew's Gospel, Barabbas was "a notorious prisoner" (Matt 27:16). He was well known to the Jewish population and to the Roman occupation police. According to Mark's Gospel, he was "imprisoned with the insurrectionists who had committed murder in the insurrection" (Mark 15:7). According to Luke's Gospel, though Jesus was accused of being "one who incites the people to rebellion" (Luke 23:5), Pilate found no evidence of that; it was Barabbas who actually *was* an insurrectionist . . . and a murderer (Luke 23:19). Peter also referred to him as a murderer (Acts 3:14). According to John's Gospel, Barabbas was also "a robber" (John 18:40).

So, Barabbas was a member of what we would now call "the resistance." He was a "freedom fighter." But, again, he was an insurrectionist, a Jewish person trying to overthrow the Roman government; he was a murderer; and he was a robber. He was a convicted, violent felon. Yet suddenly, much—no doubt—to his astonishment, Barabbas was released. Much—no doubt—to the shock and chagrin of the Roman soldiers, his death sentence was voided. He was taken off "death row" and released from the facility where he had been incarcerated. Although he was scheduled, we assume, to die by crucifixion—the method of capital punishment reserved by Rome for foreigners, slaves, and criminals, he was now a free man.

My question is this: *Whatever became of Barabbas after he was released?* No one alive today knows. But, from our limited experience and our knowledge of human nature, all of us can speculate! Using our "sanctified imagination," all of us can postulate theories regarding the immediate response of Barabbas and regarding the rest of his life. Please allow *me* to do so! There are several possibilities.

It's possible that Barabbas went out and partied. Whether for days, for weeks, or for months, he'd been in prison and out of circulation. He'd been deprived of his freedom. He'd been eating prison slop. He'd been without alcohol and drugs. It was time to eat, drink, and be merry. It was time for wine, women, and song. He'd been unable to enjoy sexual activity with his wife, his girlfriend, or with other women. He may well have had "groupies" mourning his abrupt departure from the sensual lifestyle they'd enjoyed with him prior to his arrest—groupies who never thought they'd be in his company again, groupies eager to take up with him where they'd left off at the time he was apprehended.

Certainly, he also had plenty of male friends, men with whom he'd shared the cause of the Zealots, the resistance. They would be delighted to have him back to re-invigorate their campaign, to give new impetus and leadership to their cause. They'd be ready to celebrate, to share a meal and a bottle of wine, and to make new plans together for the overthrow of Rome. If he'd been a hero to the Zealots before, he'd be all the more a hero to them now. In the most unexpected turn of events, he'd beaten the system! He'd escaped certain death! There were no longer any charges against him! He was ready to roll! To re-group! To strategize for the future! But first to *party!*

It's possible, therefore, that Barabbas returned shortly to a life of crime. Prisons rehabilitate no one. No form of punishment—including incarceration—in itself changes anyone. It can provide the context for some real soul-searching. It can give someone time to reflect on his rebellion, his sinfulness, and his unwise and wrong choices. But unless the inmate really repents of his sins, comes totally clean before God and others, cries out for forgiveness, invites the Lord to enter and take over his life, and begins walking down the path of discipleship, his lifestyle back in society will soon resemble what it was before he went to prison. In fact, sadly, even the vast majority of men and women who make commitments to Christ in American prisons in our generation backslide immediately or not long after their release—if not into a life of crime, into a life of immorality and, usually, substance abuse. At least that's the way it was in York County, Pennsylvania, where I devoted a lot of time to prison ministry, and where my wife and I spent half of our lives before moving to Arizona in January of 2009.

Even if Barabbas felt real remorse for his crimes while languishing in his prison cell, upon his release, he'd soon hear "the call of the streets"; and the lure of the world, the flesh, and the devil would inevitably prevail. For all we know, Barabbas, however altruistic he may have been, returned

31—Whatever Became of Barabbas?

to a high-risk life of crime and was killed in the streets or re-arrested, re-sentenced, and executed—as per the original intent of the judicial system. It's even possible that, following further chapters in his criminal career, he was eventually "cornered" by the police, that he barricaded himself in a house or a cave, and that—determined never to return to prison, and seeing there was no way out—he drank some poison, fell on his own sword, or otherwise committed suicide.

It's possible, on the other hand, that Barabbas really valued his totally unexpected second chance and left the resistance movement and his life of crime. It's possible, I'm saying, that he really reformed. It's possible that he "laid low"—not just until the system began to forget about him, but permanently. It's possible that he adopted a low profile, settled down, nurtured his marriage or got married—if he hadn't been previously, fathered children, became a family man, earned an honest living, and attended synagogue services on a regular basis. Though I consider this the least likely of the possibilities, his brush with death may have caused him to re-evaluate his life and priorities, decide on more peaceful means of gaining his political ends, or even drop the whole cause and simply live a quiet life out of the headlines.

It's possible—I offer a totally different scenario—*that Barabbas returned to his life of crime but much later repented and came to saving faith.* In the 1961 motion picture called "Barabbas," his escape from capital punishment because of the mob's desire for the crucifixion of Jesus of Nazareth becomes an event which haunts him the rest of his life. After watching a Christian named Rachel being stoned to death for her belief in Jesus, he returns to his life of thievery and crime. But at the end, when he himself once again faces crucifixion, he discovers genuine faith and dies a forgiven and saved man.

Well, any of these theories is plausible; any of these four scenarios may have been the one in which the life of Barabbas really played out. But there's yet another possibility, and it's my personal favorite.

It's this: *after his sudden release from prison, Barabbas may soon have become a follower of Jesus.* I would like to suggest that Barabbas soon heard rumors about Jesus' alleged resurrection from the dead and appearances to numbers of His followers and that Barabbas earnestly sought the truth about these claims. I would like to suggest that He sought out some of Jesus' followers, became convinced of the truth of Jesus' resurrection; reasoned logically back from that to the authenticity of Jesus' claim to be the Messiah, the Son of the living God; repented thoroughly of His sins, even seeing the wrongness of his attempts to bring in the kingdom of God by crime and violence; put his trust in Jesus; and set out to follow Him as part of the early church in Jerusalem!

I would like to suggest that Barabbas became a different kind of revolutionary—that, like numerous Holy-Spirit-transformed gang leaders and violent revolutionaries of our own generation, he became an evangelist to his own subculture, a leader for God and for good! I hope I'm right—for the sake of his eternal soul! Check out my rap:

> Yo, Barabbas, you got a lot of press:
> > Matt, Mark, Luke, John—nothin' but the best!
> A "notorious prisoner," an "insurrectionist,"
> > A "murderer," a "robber"—with multiple arrests.
> An angry, hostile inmate sittin' on Death Row—
> > Waitin' for that final walk, and feelin' mighty low.
> Then you got that welcome word: you had been set free!
> > Pilate let the people choose—no lawyer got a fee!
> Did you go right home when they let you out,
> > Home to your kids and wife?
> Did you burst through the door and give 'em the scoop
> > About your whole new lease on life?
> What did you say when you saw your wife
> > And told her all the news?
> Did you tell her of Jesus and His death in your place?
> > And did she get confused?
> Did she wonder how such a thing could be,
> > How your sentence got vacated?
> Did she wonder how you could still be alive,
> > Instead of decimated?
> But then what happened? Did you go out and party?
> > Did you hang with your homeboys, act not even sorry?
> Did you listen to the devil and do some more crimes?
> > Did you diss God's mercy and wallow in the slime?
> Or did you opt to reform, lay low, settle down,
> > Get out of the headlines, and stay out of town?
> Or did you blow it again, get busted and tried,
> > And repent just before you were crucified?

31—Whatever Became of Barabbas?

Or did you really sober up and start to ask some questions?
   Did you look into Jesus, check out His resurrection?
Did it dawn on you that He died in your place—
   Took the rap for *you* so your sheet could be erased?
Did you come to see the truth and repent of your sin?
   Did you leave your past behind and start to follow Him?
Did you join *His* revolution—start doin' things His way?
   Did you learn to love? Did you learn to pray?
I'm down with *that*, and I really hope it's true,
   'Cause your life was not your own, once it was given back to you.
I hope you led many to life through His death!
   I hope you served the Lord till you took your last breath!
'Cause as you found out, you gotta serve somebody—
   The devil or the Lord; the issue ain't muddy.
You can't serve two masters, only just one,
   For the rest of your life till the battle is won.
So, Barabbas, tell me, man: what road *did* you take?

Day 32

BODY PIERCING SAVED MY LIFE!

*What Thou, my Lord hast suffered
was all for sinners' gain;
Mine, mine was the transgression,
but Thine the deadly pain.*

—BERNARD OF CLAIRVAUX[1]

AS YOU KNOW, IT'S really common in our present generation for people of all sorts—street and straight, office worker and construction worker, outlaw biker and law enforcement officer, male and female, Christ-follower and unbeliever—to have tattoos and body piercings. You see tattooed people, both men and women, everywhere you go! And you see lots of body piercings too! Actually, it's not everybody; according to a Harris Poll of 2,225 U.S. adults surveyed online between October 14th and 19th in 2015, about three in ten Americans (29 percent) had at least one tattoo, up from roughly two in ten (21 percent) just four years earlier.

Actually, seven in ten (69 percent) of those with tattoos had two or more. Tattoos were especially prevalent among younger Americans, with nearly half of Millennials (47 percent) and over a third of Gen Xers (36 percent) saying they had at least one, compared to 13 percent of Baby Boomers

---

1. Bernard of Clairvaux (1092–1153), "O Sacred Head, Now Wounded," translated by James W. Alexander, First half of second verse, 1829 (public domain).

32—Body Piercing Saved My Life!

and one in ten Matures (10 percent).[2] Tattoos have become a really common sight.

So have piercings and the jewelry that goes with them. According to the "Tattoo Apprenticeship Blog," 83 percent of Americans have their ear lobes pierced, while 14 percent have body piercings elsewhere.[3] "Elsewhere" means that they're showing up on noses, eyebrows, chins, lips, tongues, navels, nipples, and even private genital areas! (No, I haven't seen any of those, but I've been told about them!) But, hey: just ask certain people to stick out their tongue or lift up their shirt or blouse a little; you'll see jewelry affixed to their tongue or their navel! Ouch!

If, by any chance, my favorite theory of what happened to Barabbas after his release from prison is true, then I know that his spirit would have resonated with what I'm about to say. Whether or not, in his identification with a revolutionary movement, he would have submitted to the piercing of his ears, his nose, his eyebrows, his tongue, or his stomach, I don't know. But surely, having seen (according to this theory) the Roman soldiers nail Jesus to that cross on Calvary, he, of all people, would have said, "Body piercing saved my life!" He might even have written that—in Jewish Aramaic, of course—on a bumper sticker and glued it to his saddlebags!

It's possible that Barabbas would have had his *ear* pierced for another reason. He was, after all, Jewish and according to the Old Testament, if a Jewish man purchased a Hebrew slave, he was obligated to release him or her after six years. If, however, the slave had come to love his or her master and enjoyed the life he provided, he or she could choose to remain a slave. The master would then take an awl and pierce it through the ear of the slave to designate permanent ownership (Deut 15:12–17).

Mary, in the New Testament, applied this concept of voluntary slavery to herself by calling herself "a bondslave of the Lord" (Luke 1:38, 48); Paul referred to Epaphras as "a bondslave of Jesus Christ" (Col 4:12); and Peter urged his believing readers, "Act as free men, and do not use your freedom as a covering for evil, but use it as bondslaves of God" (1 Pet 2:16). It's possible, therefore, that Barabbas saw himself as a bondslave of the Lord and made a point (no pun intended) of getting his ear pierced to symbolize that voluntary servitude and identify himself accordingly.

---

2. "Tattoo Takeover: Three in Ten Americans Have Tattoos, and Most Don't Stop at Just One," February 19, 2016.

3. "Statistics on Americans and Body Piercing," April 20, 2014.

In any case, it was the body piercing *Jesus* received at the hands of the Roman soldiers that resulted in the spilling of His precious blood as the atonement for our sins! Surely Barabbas would have said with Isaiah the prophet, "He was *pierced through* for our transgressions, He was crushed for our iniquities; the chastening for our well-being fell upon Him, and by His scourging we are healed. All of us like sheep have gone astray, each of us has turned to his own way; but the Lord has caused the iniquity of us all to fall on Him" (Isa 53:5–6, italics mine).

But the real question today isn't the one on Day 31: "Whatever happened to Barabbas?" It's: "Whatever happened to *you*?" Since you've learned of Jesus' body piercing and His atoning death on that awful cross for you, since you've learned of His actual resurrection from the dead, and since you've learned of His great love for you (in spite of your sin), what have you done about it? Your life *has* played out or *could* play out in a lot of different scenarios too! Which one *is* it? Which one is it *going* to be?

You may be saying, "But, dude, if I would *really* set out to follow Jesus, what would my homeboys—my friends—say??" Let me refer you to St. Peter's answer to that:

> Since Christ suffered physically, you too must strengthen yourselves with the same way of thinking that he had; because whoever suffers physically is no longer involved with sin. From now on, then, you must live the rest of your earthly lives controlled by God's will and not by human desires. You have spent enough time in the past doing what the heathen like to do. Your lives were spent in indecency, lust, drunkenness, orgies, drinking parties, and the disgusting worship of idols. And now the heathen are surprised when you do not join them in the same wild and reckless living, and so they insult you. But they will have to give an account of themselves to God, who is ready to judge the living and the dead (1 Pet 4:1–5).[4]

That puts it in perspective, doesn't it? To whom are we ultimately going to give an account, anyway?? To our "heathen" friends? Not really. To the true and living God! Has Jesus' body piercing saved *your* life? If it hasn't already, it *can*—right now!

---

4. Quotation from *Good News Translation*, Second Edition.

Day 33

Immediate Access

God waits for you to communicate with Him.
You have instant, direct access to God.
God loves mankind so much, and in a very special sense His children,
that He has made Himself available to you at all times.

—Wesley L. Duewel[1]

IN OUR COMPUTER-DRIVEN GENERATION, access is terribly important—immediate access to various websites. If, for example, we want to check our online bank statement, we need to type in our user name and our password in order to gain access. And then we can instantly see the record of our latest transactions, both deposits and withdrawals. The same is true for our e-mails and our retail purchases from web-based merchandisers like amazon.com; and, again, in most cases we need either to type in our user name and our password, or we simply count on their being saved and automatically implemented for our convenience.

The issue of access is not, however, unique to our generation. In ancient cultures and kingdoms, those who sought access to the governor or king had to follow carefully stipulated protocol. Queen Esther, for instance, risked her life by seeking an audience with King Ahasuerus, who reigned

---

1. Duewel, *Touch the World through Prayer*, 21.

over the extensive Medo-Persian Empire. Here's how the Bible describes her approach to his throne:

> Now it came about on the third day that Esther put on her royal robes and stood in the inner court of the king's palace in front of the king's rooms, and the king was sitting on his royal throne in the throne room, opposite the entrance to the palace.
> When the king saw Esther the queen standing in the court, she obtained favor in his sight; and the king extended to Esther the golden scepter which was in his hand. So Esther came near and touched the top of the scepter. Then the king said to her, "What is troubling you, Queen Esther? And what is your request? Even to half of the kingdom it shall be given to you" (Esth 5:1–3).

But there has always been a concern on the part of human beings as to how to approach their *gods*—be they deified rocks, mountains, or trees; be they deified animals, birds, or insects; or be "they" the one true and living God. And that's my concern today. How may finite and sinful human beings gain access to the presence of the infinite and holy Creator-God of the universe?

Although God has always been omnipresent, in Old Testament times—for purposes of access to Him—His presence was uniquely localized in the Holy of Holies. That was the inner sanctuary of the Tabernacle and, later, the Temple in Jerusalem where the Ark of the Covenant was kept. The Holy of Holies, which was separated from the rest of the Inner Court by a thick veil, could only be entered by the Jewish High Priest and by him only annually on Yom Kippur, the Day of Atonement. It was, therefore, a highly restricted area.

Consider this description of the veil:

> Solomon's temple was 30 cubits high (1 Kings 6:2), but Herod had increased the height to 40 cubits, according to the writings of Josephus, a first century Jewish historian. There is uncertainty as to the exact measurement of a cubit, but it is safe to assume that this veil was somewhere near 60 feet high. Josephus also tells us that the veil was four inches thick and that horses tied to each side could not pull the veil apart. The book of Exodus teaches that this thick veil was fashioned from blue, purple and scarlet material and fine twisted linen.[2]

---

2. From website: *Got Questions?org*.

33 — Immediate Access

As we've seen previously, certain startling and amazing events took place at the moment of Jesus' death on the cross. Here's how Matthew recounts them:

> And Jesus cried out again with a loud voice, and yielded up His spirit. And behold, the veil of the temple was torn in two from top to bottom; and the earth shook and the rocks were split. The tombs were opened, and many bodies of the saints who had fallen asleep [i.e., died] were raised; and coming out of the tombs after His resurrection they entered the holy city and appeared to many (Matt 27:51–53, brackets mine).

I want today to dwell simply on one of those events: "the veil of the temple was torn in two from top to bottom." Think this through with me. The sixty-foot-high, four-inch thick veil of the temple was suddenly torn in two, and it was torn from top to bottom. This event was completely unprecedented, totally unexpected, and absolutely inexplicable—apart from some sort of supernatural act, some sort of divine intervention. The timing of this supernatural phenomenon was no accident or coincidence; it occurred, you'll notice, at the moment of Jesus' expiration. Surely *God* did this, whether by baring His mighty arm or through assigning it to one or more of His holy angels. Since God doesn't perform signs and wonders to amuse or entertain us or to "show off" His omnipotence, this unique intervention in the long-standing status of things in His Temple must have some deep, even cosmic, meaning.

It does! Let me try to run it down for you. The splitting of the veil at the moment Jesus took His last breath . . .

- Demonstrated that His spilled blood was sufficient as an atonement for the sins of mankind (Heb 9:11–14);
- Showed that God would never again dwell in a material temple made with human hands (Acts 17:24);
- Indicated that "the Lamb of God" had rendered the entire Jewish religious system and all of its elements—such as the Temple itself, the priesthood, the animal sacrifices, the grain offerings, and the incense—obsolete, in that they had found their fulfillment in Him (Heb 9:1–12);
- Established Jesus as our Great High Priest and as the only way to God (Heb 4:14; 6:19–20; 7:26–8);

- Declared that the New Covenant had now superseded and replaced the Old Covenant (Heb 8:7–13; 9:15–28);
- Announced that the barrier between Jew and Gentile was also torn down for all who put their trust in Jesus as Lord, God, and Messiah (Eph 2:11–18); and
- Signified that the Holy of Holies was open now, not just for the Jewish High Priest on one day of the year, but for all believers at any time of the year and at any moment of the day!

Let's refresh our souls with Scriptures that so wonderfully document that last point. First: St. Paul mentions "the eternal purpose which [God the Father] carried out in Christ Jesus our Lord, in whom we have boldness and *confident access* [to God] through faith in Him" (Eph 3:11–12, italics and brackets mine). Then the writer of the Epistle to the Hebrews (Jewish believers in Jesus, the Messiah) concludes:

> Therefore, since we have a great high priest who has passed through the heavens, Jesus the Son of God, let us hold fast our confession. For we do not have a high priest who cannot sympathize with our weaknesses, but One who has been tempted in all things as we are, yet without sin. Therefore let us *draw near with confidence to the throne of grace*, so that we may receive mercy and find grace to help in time of need (Heb 4:14–16, italics mine).
>
> Therefore, brethren, since we have *confidence to enter the holy place* by the blood of Jesus, by a new and living way which He inaugurated for us through the veil, that is, His flesh, and since we have a great priest over the house of God, let us *draw near* with a sincere heart in full assurance of faith, having our hearts sprinkled clean from an evil conscience and our bodies washed with pure water (Heb 10:19–22, italics mine).

Notice that, if we're to draw near with expectation of access to the Throne, our hearts are to be cleansed from an evil conscience. Awhile back, I was reading Psalm 24, where David asks in verse 3, "Who may ascend into the hill of the LORD? And who may stand in His holy place?" He answers his own question in verse 4: "He who has clean hands and a pure heart, who has not lifted up his soul to falsehood and has not sworn deceitfully." Fiona Barnard explains:

> In Psalm 24, the pilgrim people of God are conscious that they are traveling to Jerusalem, to go to the Temple for an audience with

33—Immediate Access

the King of kings. They want to praise him and prepare themselves appropriately. This means far more than being smartly dressed or observing court protocol. For this King cares about right living, inside as well as out, about the state of our hearts and not just our appearance. Under such scrutiny, each of us falls short and needs the grace that only God can provide to allow us to stand in his presence. But when we do come in the right spirit, we can be assured of an audience with the King.[3]

Wow! Immediate access to the throne room of the triune God in heaven—for you, for me! What's the "user name"? Your own given name! What's the "password"? "Blood" (the blood of Jesus)! Let's take advantage of it on a daily basis! Let's prize His Passion! Let's draw near!

---

3. Barnard, "Behold Your King," *Encounter with God*, Jul/Aug/Sep 2016, 63.

Day 34

The Greatest Rescue

From sinking sand He lifted me,
With tender hand He lifted me;
From shades of night to plains of light,
Oh, praise His Name, He lifted me!

—*Charles H. Gabriel*[1]

WE REFER FREQUENTLY TO "the gospel of Jesus Christ." But what *is* the gospel? What does that term include? Well, quite clearly, it includes *good* news; in fact, the word "gospel" comes from the old-English word which *means* "good news." As St. Paul explains,

> Now I make known to you, brethren, the *gospel* which I preached to you, which also you received, in which also you stand, by which also you are saved, if you hold fast the word which I preached to you, unless you believed in vain. For I delivered to you as of first importance what I also received, that *Christ died for our sins* according to the Scriptures, and that *He was buried*, and that *He was raised on the third day* according to the Scriptures, and that He *appeared* to Cephas [St. Peter], and then to the twelve [all of the original apostles—minus Judas] (1 Cor 15:1–4, italics and brackets mine).

---

1. Gabriel, "He Lifted Me," Chorus, 1905 (public domain).

But I noticed some time ago that "the gospel" includes something else: *bad* news. Listen to *these* words from St. Paul:

> But the [Mosaic] Law [containing the Ten Commandments] is good, if one uses it lawfully, realizing the fact that the law [*any law made for the welfare of the population of a particular society*] is not made for a righteous person, but for those who are sinners, for the unholy and profane, for those who kill their fathers or mothers, for murderers and immoral men and homosexuals and kidnappers and liars and perjurers, and whatever else is contrary to sound teaching, according to the glorious *gospel* of the blessed God, with which I have been entrusted (1 Tim 1:8-11, brackets and italics mine).

So, according to Paul in 1 Corinthians, "the gospel" includes in the *forefront* the *good* news of the death (on a Roman cross), the burial (in a borrowed tomb), and the resurrection (from that tomb) of Jesus of Nazareth. It also includes the documentation of His resurrection by eyewitnesses. But, according to Paul in 1 Timothy, "the gospel" includes something else: a *backdrop* of *bad* news: our failure to keep the Law of God, our rebellion, our transgressions, our disobedience to God, our waywardness, and the contradiction of our behavior, our attitudes, and our speech to sound teaching. It includes the extent, the magnitude, and the seriousness of our *sin*. In other words, "the gospel" includes the *bad* news as well as the *good* news.

In fact, if it weren't for the *bad* news, there'd be no need for the *good* news. If we hadn't been dirty, rotten, lousy, no-good sinners,[2] Jesus would

---

2. Have you gotten used to my describing us like that? I realize it's not very flattering, but I don't intend it to be. Sometimes, people view sin as simply a list of behaviors in which we ought not to participate: "I don't smoke, and I don't chew [tobacco], and I don't go with the girls who do!" But we dare not trivialize sin, for that in itself is an extremely serious matter (1 Kgs 16:31). So, what is sin? Biblically, sin can be defined in several ways: (1) breaking the law, doing what is expressly forbidden by God (1 John 3:4); (2) failing to do what is right, neglecting to do what is expressly commanded by God (Jas 4:17); (3) failing to measure up to the standard of perfection God has established in His law and in the life of Christ (Rom 3:23); (4) doing our own thing, living according to self-will and self-centeredness (Isa 53:6a); and (5) unbelief in Jesus Christ (John 16:8-9). Sin pervades human life from the cradle to the grave (Ps 51:5; Prov 24:9; 22:15; Gen 8:21; Jer 17:9; Mark 7:21-23; Rom 7:18; Eccl 12:1), and it's humanly incurable (Jer 30:12-13, 15; Job 14:4; 25:4; Jer 13:23), even by religious rituals and self-energized good works (Eph 2:8-9; Titus 3:5-7). As we're all learning by one public scandal after another, even our most private sins—if not brought voluntarily into the light of the Lord, confessed before Him, and forsaken (1 John 1:5-10)—will eventually be exposed, "find us out," as the Scripture says (Num 32:23). We should be fearful of sinning (1 Tim 5:19-20; Heb 10:26-31).

not have had to leave heaven for earth, let alone go to the cross to spill His life's blood to atone for our sins. We ignore this aspect of the gospel, minimize it, dilute it, or repudiate it to our own peril or that of other people with whom we interact and to whom we try to represent the Savior. If we aren't in serious trouble, why do we need a Savior?

The drama began at 2:30 on a Saturday afternoon, December 5, 1970. As reported shortly thereafter by *The Denver Post*, a man named Pat Garvey was looking for interesting rocks near an old mine shaft just north of Central City, Colorado. He was accompanied by his ninety-five-pound, white German Shepherd named Shelley. "The dog was on one side of the open shaft and Garvey on the other when Garvey called him," according to staff writer Bill Myers. But "Shelley got too close [while] skirting the hole and fell in. Garvey called repeatedly but got no answer. He finally gave him up for dead because the hole [was] 400 feet deep."

"But during the night Garvey decided to go to the shaft again on Sunday in case the dog merely had been knocked unconscious. Sure enough, he heard Shelley whining from deep within the shaft. The dog would bark when Garvey called his name. Garvey went back to town for help;" and Bill Russell, the Mayor of Central City, and Norm Blake, the Deputy State Commissioner of Mines, responded. The Commissioner himself came to the shaft and, at great personal risk, allowed himself to be lowered by the Mayor in an old, one-ton ore-bucket to the one-hundred-ten-foot level, where he found Shelley in total darkness on a shelf where he'd landed. Shelley was frightened but, amazingly, was without serious injury. He "hopped into the bucket with Blake and bathed him with gratitude all the way up"![3]

Think about it: you and I have fallen into the shaft of sin. But God heard our faint whimper and sent Jesus Christ, His Son, to the scene of our fall. Jesus has come—at what we now call the first Christmas, and at great personal risk has allowed Himself to be lowered through His birth as a human being and then through His death as a common criminal—on what we now call Good Friday—to the one-hundred-ten-foot level, to the seventy-five-foot level, to the twenty-five-foot level, to the five-foot level, or to the very bottom of the shaft, depending on where we, individually, have been in the depths of disobedience and sinfulness. He has encouraged us to hop into the heavenly ore bucket and allowed us to pour out our hearts

---

3. Bill Myers, "Dog Plucked to Safety After Mine Shaft Plunge," *Denver Post*, December 8, 1970, page unknown by me.

34—The Greatest Rescue

in gratitude as He's taken us out of the shaft and planted our feet on solid ground!

King David testified to something very similar to this in the first three verses of Psalm 40:

> I waited patiently for the Lord;
>   And He inclined to me and heard my cry.
> He brought me up out of the pit of destruction, out of the miry clay,
>   And He set my feet upon a rock making my footsteps firm.
> He put a new song in my mouth, a song of praise to our God;
>   Many will see and fear and will trust in the Lord.

Can you give the same sort of testimony? Has the rescue happened yet to you? Have you climbed into the heavenly ore bucket and let Jesus rescue you? Have your feet been planted on solid ground?

Day 35

No Place in Me

*The strength of a man's virtue
should not be measured by his special exertions,
but by his habitual acts.*

—BLAISE PASCAL[1]

WE NEED TO UNDERSTAND that there was an extreme, hard-fought conflict between Jesus Christ and Satan throughout Jesus' life on earth. When Jesus was a toddler, Satan, working through King Herod (as we've seen previously), tried to kill Him during the slaughter of the children in and around Bethlehem (Matt 2:7–18; Rev 12:3–4). When He was about to begin His earthly ministry at the age of thirty, Satan, working directly, offered Him three major temptations at the end of His forty days of fasting in the wilderness (Matt 4:1–11), all of which would have diverted Him from His mission. And throughout His life and ministry on earth, Satan, working through a variety of circumstances and persons, tempted Him in all the clever, shrewd, and sneaky ways in which we are tempted (Heb 4:15).

But Jesus never sinned. He never gave in. He steadfastly resisted the attempted intrusions of His archenemy into His life. He resolutely staved off the assaults of the adversary upon His holiness, His purity, and His obedience to the Father. Even His human enemies were unable, when challenged

---

1. Pascal, *Pensees*, page unknown by me.

35—No Place in Me

by Him, to convict Him of sin (John 8:46). The Pharisees, in an attempt to trap Him, admitted that they knew He was truthful, taught the way of God in truth, deferred to no one (i.e., courted no man's favor), and was not partial to anyone (Matt 22:16). Peter, who lived in close companionship with Him for three solid years, later testified that He "committed no sin, nor was any deceit found in His mouth, and even while [He was] being reviled [during His Passion], He did not revile in return; while suffering, He uttered no threats, but kept entrusting Himself to Him who judges righteously" (1 Pet 2:22–23, brackets mine).

Jesus was able to say, "I have overcome the world" (John 16:33). In other words, "I have steadfastly resisted its attempts to squeeze Me into its own mold, entice Me to adopt its own value-system, drag Me into the muck and mire of its sin and debauchery, and demean Me by getting Me to retaliate in kind to its abusive treatment of Me." Yet the conflict was intense, and it was real. And it culminated on the night before His crucifixion, the night of His betrayal by Judas.

On the occasion of His last supper with His twelve disciples—in fact, at the conclusion of that meal, Jesus said, "I will not speak much more with you, for the ruler of the world is coming" (John 14:30). He was referring to Satan, for St. Paul later referred to Satan as "the god of this world" (2 Cor 4:4), and St. John stated bluntly toward the end of his life that "the whole world lies in the power of the evil one" (1 John 5:19). Satan, even now (but hopefully not for long!), is indeed the ruler of the world.

But how was he coming at this point in time? Among other vehicles of evil expression and intent, he was coming, tragically, through one of the Twelve—through Judas Iscariot, who was shortly to betray Jesus into the hands of His enemies, who, in turn, would press for His execution by Roman crucifixion. But how in the world was Satan able to come through Judas? Because, even though Judas was a member of Jesus' disciple band and therefore what we would now call "a professing Christian," he had opened a door to Satan well before this. Follow the "trail" here.

You may recall that St. Paul advises, "Be angry, and yet do not sin; do not let the sun go down on your anger, and do not give the devil an opportunity [literally, do not give the devil place]. Let him who steals, steal no longer..." (Eph 4:26–28, brackets mine). And St. John reveals that Judas "was a thief, and as he had the money box [for Jesus' disciple band], he used to pilfer what was put into it" (John 12:6, brackets mine). Probably long before He became a follower of Jesus, he had begun to steal money and possessions from other people, perhaps even his parents or his siblings at home and possibly vendors in the marketplace.

And even though he now followed Jesus, he still engaged in his long-standing habit of stealing. He had long since given the devil an opportunity. He had long since opened that area of his life to the enemy and given him place. And he didn't stop doing it even though he was regularly in the presence of the Son of God. You can be sure, too, that if it was his habit to steal, it was also his habit to lie—in order to cover up. That's the way sin works. One sin leads to another to another to another to another until he who commits sin is the slave of sin (John 8:34).

St. John states that the devil had "*already* [before Jesus' last celebration of the Passover with His disciples] *put into the heart* of Judas Iscariot, the son of Simon, to betray Him" (John 13:2, italics and brackets mine)—to sell Jesus into the hands of His enemies. Question: how could Satan possibly have gained access to the heart of one of Jesus' disciples? Answer: he had access to it long before—through the simple sins of stealing and lying. In a chilling additional detail, John records that after Jesus dipped a morsel and gave it to Judas, "Satan then *entered* into him," and Jesus said, "What you do, do quickly" (John 13:27, italics mine).

William Makepeace Thackeray was right when he said, "Sow a thought, reap an act. Sow an act, reap a habit. Sow a habit, reap a character. Sow a character, reap an eternal destiny." Judas began many years before to steal and lie. He thereby gave the devil place—an opening, an opportunity. Satan maximized that opportunity and exploited that place that he'd taken over in Judas's life. Later, because of Judas's greed and penchant for ill-gotten gain, Satan was able to put the thought in his heart to betray Jesus—for thirty pieces of silver, one-hundred-twenty days' wages (the earnings of just under one-third of a year). Still later, he was able to enter him to control the very consummation of the wicked scheme he'd engineered—the scheme that required skulduggery, deception, greed, and treason.

The ruler of the world was coming, all right, as Jesus had said; but, in that same verse, Jesus was able to say, "he has nothing in Me" (John 14:30). By conspicuous contrast with Judas, Jesus could say, "[Satan] has nothing in Me." Other translators and commentators suggest these insightful options:

- "He has no claim on Me" (*Amplified Bible* and *English Standard Version*).
- "He has nothing in common with Me" (*Amplified Bible*).

35—No Place in Me

- "He has no power over Me" *(Amplified Bible)*.
- "He has no hold over Me" *(New International Version)*.
- "There is nothing in Me that belongs to him" *(Amplified Bible)*.
- "There is nothing in Me in sympathy with him" *(Barnes' Notes on the New Testament)*.
- "There is nothing in Me he can call his" *(Barnes' Notes on the New Testament)*.

In other words (I would suggest), "There is no sin-caused weakness in Me for Satan to exploit, to take advantage of." As Merrill Tenney observes, "There was nothing in Jesus' character or action that could be used against him. Satan had no valid accusation that could be used as leverage to divert Jesus from the will of his Father. His obedience had been perfect, and he intended to complete the Father's purpose irrespective of what it might cost him."[2] Jesus had never, even for a moment, provided an opportunity for the devil; He had never given place to him. He had never succumbed to temptation, never opened His heart and life to the enemy. If only *we* could say that! Remember: He was tempted in every way Judas was, in every way you and I are—even to steal and lie; but He never gave in, He never sinned. He lived exclusively to do the will of His Father who sent Him.

Do you want to be like Jesus or like Judas? Does Satan have no place in you, or does he have an opportunity in you? Have you maintained a resolute commitment to the Father to do His will, or are there areas of your mind, heart, and life still open to the devil? Are you steadfastly resisting temptation, or are you coddling and/or trying to hide a certain sin? Are you totally open to the statutes and standards of the Lord, or are you trying to rationalize and justify a particular transgression? Are you pressing on in total obedience to the Lord, or are you blatantly refusing to submit to His will in a particular area of your life?

Are you harboring bitterness, resentment, and hatred toward another human being or even God Himself? Are you filled with greed and covetousness? Are you filled with lust and lasciviousness? Like Judas, are you—in any application of the terms—pilfering or stealing anything from anyone (including the government)? Are you involved in any sneaking around,

---

2. Tenney, *The Expositor's Bible Commentary with the New International Version of The Holy Bible*, Volume 9, 149.

lying, deception, or cover-up? Are you doing any cheating, rule-breaking, or law-breaking?

If so, isn't it about time you dealt with these matters before God, repented of them, and sought His forgiveness and cleansing and deliverance? Isn't it about time you sought His strength to live a new life, free from these potential and actual bondages? Isn't it about time you made a clean break with your sin?

Day 36

The Stigmata

*We need men of the cross, with the message of the cross,
bearing the marks of the cross.*

—*Vance Havner*[1]

SOMETIMES WE MAY THINK doctrine is not all that important. Indeed, we do well to avoid useless theological discussions—e.g., about how many angels can dance on the head of a pin. At some point, we need even to terminate our debates over the tenets of Calvinists vs. those of Arminians.[2] For one thing, we're not likely to change the mind of our "opponent," and, for another, we may be wasting precious time in the effort—time that could much better be spent in sharing the gospel with those who don't yet believe or in encouraging fellow-believers in their walk with the Lord.

There *is* reason, however, to "contend earnestly for the faith that was once for all handed down to the saints" (Jude 3). Jude, a former skeptic and the half-brother of our Lord, said that; and he ought to know. He's referring to the "non-negotiables"—the core truths, the essential elements of the

---

1. Havner, *Day by Day with Vance Havner: 366 Devotions*, devotion for May 5, page unknown by me.
2. Don't be sidetracked by these names if you're not familiar with them. To oversimplify, Calvinists lay heavier stress on the sovereignty of God in salvation, while Arminians lay heavier stress on the free will of man. Both groups have valid theological points to make and multiple Scriptures to undergird them.

gospel, those doctrines that earnest scholars of a century ago called "the fundamentals of the faith." The writer of the Epistle to the Hebrews echoes Jude's concern:

> . . . we must pay much closer attention to what we have heard, *so that we do not drift away from it.* For if the word spoken through angels proved unalterable, and every transgression and disobedience received a just penalty, how will we escape if we *neglect* so great a salvation? After it was at the first spoken through the Lord, it was confirmed to us by those who heard, God also testifying with them, both by signs and wonders and by various miracles and by gifts of the Holy Spirit according to His own will (Heb 2:1-4, italics mine).

And, of course, Paul repeatedly stresses his passionate concern along these lines. He exhorts Timothy, "Be diligent to present yourself approved to God as a workman who does not need to be ashamed, *accurately handling the word of truth*" (2 Tim 2:15, italics mine). He urges him, "Preach the word; be ready in season and out of season; reprove, rebuke, exhort, with great patience and instruction. For the time will come when they will not endure sound doctrine; but wanting to have their ears tickled, they will accumulate for themselves teachers in accordance to their own desires, and will turn away their ears from the truth and will turn aside to myths" (2 Tim 4:2-4).

His writings on this subject can get even stronger! To the church at Galatia he writes:

> I am amazed that you are so quickly deserting Him who called you by the grace of Christ, for a different gospel; which is really not another; only there are some who are disturbing you and want to distort the gospel of Christ. But even if we, or an angel from heaven, should preach to you a gospel contrary to what we have preached to you, he is to be accursed! As we have said before, so I say again now, if any man is preaching to you a gospel contrary to what you received, he is to be accursed! For am I now seeking the favor of men, or of God? Or am I striving to please men? If I were still trying to please men, I would not be a bond-servant of Christ (Gal 1:6-10) . . . I wish that those who are troubling you would even mutilate [castrate] themselves (Gal 5:12, brackets mine).

Whoa! That's really strong! But it *should* be! Why? Because (and this was the error into which many of the Galatian believers had fallen) if we are not saved by grace alone through faith alone, and if we must add certain human rituals (such as circumcision) or "works" to our faith in order to be saved,

36—The Stigmata

then we have nullified the grace of God, blasphemed and rendered unnecessary the work of Christ on the cross, and fatally compromised the gospel itself. And that's why I bring this matter to your attention in a volume on the Passion of our Lord.

You see, it all comes down to what happened on the cross, why it happened, and what was accomplished there. Paul puts it in context here:

> Those who desire to make a good showing in the flesh try to compel you to be circumcised, simply so that they will not be persecuted for the cross of Christ. For those who are circumcised do not even keep the Law themselves, but they desire to have you circumcised so that they may boast in your flesh. But may it never be that I would boast, except in the cross of our Lord Jesus Christ, through which the world has been crucified to me, and I to the world. For neither is circumcision anything, nor uncircumcision, but a new creation (Gal 6:12–15).

Do you see the inseparable connection between doctrine and salvation? Do you grasp the critical nature of the theological issue at stake? Do you perceive the life-and-death difference between (a) salvation by the grace of God through faith in Jesus Christ and (b) salvation through a belief-system *and* human works, between (a) the efficacy of the cross of Christ and (b) the efforts of the flesh? Obviously, Paul did. In fact, his unshakeable stand for the truth—for the simplicity and purity of the gospel—provoked much of the persecution he experienced, even the physical abuse he received. That's why he went on to say, "And those who will walk by this rule, peace and mercy be upon them, and upon the Israel of God. From now on let no one cause trouble for me, for I bear on my body the brand-marks of Jesus" (Gal 6:16–17).

The original Greek word translated "brand-marks" in English is *stigmata*. *Stigmata* are marks pricked in or branded on someone's body. In the Roman Empire, slaves and soldiers bore the name or the stamp of their master or commander branded or cut into their bodies to indicate the one to whom they belonged. Paul, who considered himself a bondslave of Jesus Christ (as previously noted), proudly referenced his *stigmata* in this passage, calling them the *"stigmata of Jesus."*

The differences, however, between his *stigmata* and those of actual slaves or soldiers were that his were inflicted involuntarily, were received in the context of abuse and torture, and were imposed with no decorative design or crafted brand. They came from innumerable miscellaneous

Prizing His Passion

beatings, three beatings with rods, one stoning, and five vicious whippings with thirty-nine brutal lashes each time (2 Cor 11:23–25)—administered with leather strands containing embedded pieces of metal or bone near their ends. And these represented just *a portion* of the price Paul paid for his passion for truth and his irrevocable commitment to the One who had apprehended him, loved him, forgiven him, transformed him, and called him into service as an ambassador for His kingdom.

Over the nearly two millennia of church history since the first century, many individuals, primarily Roman Catholic in affiliation, have claimed supernaturally to have received bleeding wounds similar to those inflicted on Jesus—on their brow, back, wrists, feet, and chest. Others have even inflicted such wounds on themselves. It's not my purpose to comment on the legitimacy of the claims of the former or to comment on the wisdom of the latter. I simply want to say that these so-called "stigmata" have absolutely nothing to do with those of the Apostle Paul. He never claimed to have wounds on his body that paralleled Jesus' actual wounds, nor did he claim that his wounds somehow mysteriously and supernaturally appeared on his body, nor did he inflict them on himself.

He received them in random fashion at the instigation of religious leaders, political leaders, and merchants whose vested interests were threatened. He didn't seek them, nor did he enjoy them; but, in an appropriate way, he was proud of them and offered them as proof of his divine call and his authentic apostleship.

How much do you suffer for your faith in Christ? How much do I? I've taken periodic flak (only once of a slightly physical nature) in various ways over the years for my stand for Him, for truth, and for righteousness; but nothing I've experienced remotely compares to what Paul endured or what our brethren in many parts of the world are currently experiencing. How important is cross-centered sound doctrine to *us*? What price are *we* willing to pay to maintain our commitment to it?

Day 37

Room at the Cross

I asked Jesus, "How much do You love me?"
"This much," He answered.
Then He stretched out His arms . . . and died.

—Author Unknown

God has made room for *you*—at the cross. St. Paul proclaimed: "God demonstrates His own love toward us, in that while we were yet sinners, Christ died for us [on the cross]" (Rom 5:8, brackets mine). As we've seen more than once, he testified: "I have been crucified with Christ; and it is no longer I who live, but Christ lives in me; and the life which I now live in the flesh I live by faith in the Son of God, who loved me and gave Himself up for me [on the cross]" (Gal 2:20, brackets mine).

He explained: "Christ redeemed us from the curse of the Law, having become a curse for us—for it is written, 'CURSED IS EVERYONE WHO HANGS ON A TREE' [in this case, the cross—made of wood from a tree]—in order that in Christ Jesus the blessing of Abraham might come to the Gentiles, so that we would receive the promise of the Spirit through faith" (Gal 3:13-14, brackets mine). And he added: "There is neither Jew nor Greek, there is neither slave nor free man, there is neither male nor female; for you are all one in Christ Jesus. And if you belong to Christ, then you are Abraham's descendants, heirs according to promise" (Gal 3:28-29).

Think about the truths contained in these verses! You don't have to be *good* to be included. As a matter of fact, to get into His kingdom, you have to admit you're *not* good, that you're a sinner who has miserably failed to measure up to God's standard of perfection. You need to cry out for His mercy and forgiveness and cleansing. He'll impute to you, then, *His* righteousness and *His* goodness and declare you acquitted of your transgressions against Him! You don't have to be a *Jew* to be included. If you, as a *Gentile*, have put your trust in the Jewish Messiah, the blessing of Abraham has come to you! You don't have to be *rich* to be included. If you belong to Christ by faith, even if you are *poor*, you are one with the rich in Christ! You don't have to be *male* to be included. If you're a believer in Jesus and you're *female*, unlike the situation in certain other religions, you're on a par with male believers! God has made room for *you*—at the cross. He has included you in His plan; and, if you've come to Him in repentance and faith, He has included you in His family!

And that's just it: through repentance and faith, you should make room for *Him*—in your heart. By that I mean two things. First, you should *invite* Him into your heart, if you've never yet done so. In a scenario described by the risen, ascended, and exalted Christ Himself, He was standing outside the lives of professing believers, self-deluded members of the church in Laodicea in Asia Minor (now Turkey)—people who thought, in their spiritual apathy and pride, that they were in good shape with God. And He was saying to them, "Behold, I stand at the door and knock; if anyone hears My voice and opens the door, I will come in to him and will dine with him, and he with Me" (Rev 3:20). He wants to sit down across the dining-room table of your heart from you and have fellowship with you.

You need to understand that in Middle Eastern culture—and Jesus, of course, was Middle Eastern—hospitality was and is terribly important, to be invited to a meal in someone's house or apartment or in a Bedouin's tent is no small thing, and to eat with Middle-Easterners at their table (or in some cases, cross-legged on the floor) is not a hurried affair. People take time to eat together, to talk together earnestly as well as light-heartedly, and to enjoy each other's company. The neighboring, Arabic, Roman Catholic family that befriended my daughter and her colleague during their first year of language study in the Middle Eastern country that is now their home invited them and my wife and me over for dinner during our visit in the spring of 2004.

37—Room at the Cross

It was quite an honor and quite an experience! Bassam is Palestinian and his wife Faiza is Jordanian. He spoke English quite well; she spoke no English! It was interesting, by the way, to observe my daughter and her fellow-student conversing in Arabic with Faiza and her children and other relatives during the meal. Their conversation was animated, as was mine with Bassam; and mine was at times intense. Bassam and Faiza served us one course after another of delicious Arabic food: salads, bread, vegetables, marinated beef on a skewer, chicken and rice, cookies, water, mango juice, and soda—more food than we could possibly eat in one sitting. The meal probably lasted two to two-and-a-half hours! So, when Jesus indicated He wanted to come in and "dine" with individuals, He had something in-depth in mind.

But, once you've invited Jesus into your heart and life, you should also *allow Him to be at home* there. Paul prays for the believers in Ephesus "that He [God] would grant you, according to the riches of His glory, to be strengthened with power through His Spirit in the inner man, so that Christ may *dwell in your hearts* through faith" (Eph 3:16–17, italics mine). That word "dwell" literally means "to settle down and be at home," so Paul is concerned that we allow Christ to settle down and be at home in our hearts.

Moved by this verse, Presbyterian Pastor Robert Boyd Munger many years ago wrote a wonderful little booklet entitled, *My Heart, Christ's Home*. In that booklet he imagined Jesus not just being invited into the heart of the believer, but being allowed to settle down and be at home in every room of the house that is the believer's life—to take control of every area of his or her life. Allow me to ask: does Jesus have full access to your "library," your "kitchen," your "living room," your "dining room," your "bedroom," your "den," your "recreation room," your "basement," your "attic," and your "closets"?

He has made room for *you*—at the cross. You should make room for *Him*—in your heart!

Day 38

CLEAN!

He breaks the power of cancelled sin,
He sets the prisoner free;
His blood can make the foulest clean;
His blood availed for me.

—CHARLES WESLEY[1]

I WANT TO RETURN today to the events of the night before Jesus' crucifixion, to the outset of the last Passover He would celebrate with His disciples, to the upper room and that familiar but astonishing scene where He washed His disciples' feet. We've already pondered on Day 2 the anomaly of deity washing humanity's feet. But here's the part I want to probe today:

> Then He poured water into the basin, and began to wash the disciples' feet and to wipe them with the towel with which He was girded. So He came to Simon Peter. He said to Him, "Lord, do You wash my feet?" Jesus answered and said to him, "What I do you do not realize now, but you will understand hereafter." Peter said to Him, "Never shall You wash my feet!" Jesus answered him, "If I do not wash you, you have no part with Me." Simon Peter said to Him, "Lord, then wash not only my feet, but also my hands and my head." Jesus said to him, "He who has bathed needs only to

---

1. Wesley, "O for a Thousand Tongues to Sing," Verse 4, 1739 (public domain).

38—Clean!

wash his feet, but is completely clean; and you are clean, but not all of you." For He knew the one who was betraying Him; for this reason He said, "Not all of you are clean" (John 13:5-11).

The last part is pretty easy to understand: all of Jesus' disciples were "clean" except Judas Iscariot, whose heart was still dirty—including with his plans to betray Jesus into the hands of His enemies that very night. We contemplated Judas' treachery on Day 35. But what can we learn from Jesus' interaction with *Peter* on this occasion? Like many of us, Peter has a habit of not "getting it" and, worse, sticking his foot in his mouth. This is yet another example of that.

He is totally resistant to the idea of Jesus suddenly assuming the role of a household slave. Never mind that Peter—or one of his compatriots—should have assumed that role himself. On the one hand, Peter was right: someone other than Jesus *should* have undertaken this business of foot-washing on that fateful night. On the other hand, it hadn't occurred to him that he himself could have volunteered. But that's not the deeper issue here.

First Peter protests. Then Jesus explains that if he refuses to allow Him to wash his feet, he has no part with Him—he effectively disassociates himself from Him. Shocked by such a prospect, Peter overdoes it: he asks Jesus to wash his hands and his head too! Jesus says that's not necessary, because Peter has already bathed and is—except for his feet—completely clean. Does that mean Peter had taken a bath before he showed up in the upper room for the feast? Not really. Whether he had done so or not we don't know; but that's not Jesus' point.

Jesus indicates that—except for Judas Iscariot—all His disciples have "bathed" and are completely clean. They need only their feet to be washed. Although some commentators feel He is referencing water baptism, I do not. Surely, what He's saying is that, upon their repentance and their expression of faith in Him, He has already forgiven and cleansed them of the contamination of sin. He would explain later that same evening, "You are already clean because of the word which I have spoken to you" (John 15:3). And Paul would later declare, "Therefore there is now no condemnation for those who are in Christ Jesus" (Rom 8:1). Paul would also write, "In Him we have redemption through His blood, the forgiveness of our trespasses, according to the riches of His grace which He lavished on us" (Eph 1:7-8).

In other words, when a person turns from his sin, embraces Jesus as his Sin-Bearer, is born of His Spirit, and is granted the free gift of eternal life, he (or she, of course) is forgiven and cleansed of *all* his sins—past, present, and future. He receives a spiritual bath in the blood of Jesus, (I say it reverently) the heavenly detergent. The issue then becomes one not of losing and needing to regain his *salvation* but of losing and needing to regain his *fellowship* with God.

Sinful thoughts, words, and deeds cause loss of fellowship and require confession and repentance—in other words, a "foot-washing." The offender is basically a saved, forgiven, and cleansed person, but he has dirtied his conscience and his mind, mouth, or body with a specific sin, and he needs to be cleansed of it in order to restore fellowship with God—to keep the lines of communication open. As John, who was present during the whole scenario in the upper room and who indeed recorded it for us, would explain when he wrote to fellow-believers decades later,

> This is the message we have heard from Him and announce to you, that God is Light, and in Him there is no darkness at all. If we say that we have fellowship with Him and yet walk in the darkness, we lie and do not practice the truth; but if we walk in the Light as He Himself is in the Light, we have fellowship with one another, and the blood of Jesus His Son cleanses us from all sin. If we say that we have no sin, we are deceiving ourselves and the truth is not in us. If we confess our sins, He is faithful and righteous to forgive us our sins and to cleanse us from all unrighteousness. If we say that we have not sinned, we make Him a liar and His word is not in us (1 John 1:5–10).[2]

There's even a biblical prayer geared toward unearthing sins we may have missed: "Search me, O God, and know my heart; try me and know my anxious thoughts; and see if there be any hurtful way in me, and lead me in the everlasting way" (Ps 139:23–24, stripped by me of its poetic structure). And there's even a biblical invitation to experience a cleansing transformation, and it's from the Lord Himself. It's in the Old Testament, in Isaiah 1:18: "'Come now, and let us reason together,' says the LORD, 'Though your sins are as scarlet, they will be as white as snow; though they are red like crimson, they will be like wool.'"

Thus, the big questions for you as you read this today are these:

- Have you been bathed, spiritually, in the blood of Jesus, thereby experiencing the forgiveness of all your sins—past, present, and future?

---

2. Quoted previously on Day 10.

38—Clean!

- Are you getting your spiritual feet washed in His blood on a regular basis through walking in the Light and consistently confessing any sins exposed by that Light?
- In fact, is there any sin that you need to bring before the throne of grace right now? It's inestimably important to keep short accounts with God. It's indescribably liberating to be clean before Him!

James Nicholson, in his time-honored hymn, captured what should be the consistent cry of our hearts:

> Lord Jesus, I long to be perfectly whole;
>   I want Thee forever to live in my soul;
> Break down every idol, cast out every foe—
>   Now wash me, and I shall be whiter than snow.
> Lord Jesus, let nothing unholy remain,
>   Apply Thine own blood and extract every stain;
> To get this blest cleansing, I all things forego—
>   Now wash me, and I shall be whiter than snow.
> Lord Jesus, look down from Thy throne in the skies,
>   And help me to make a complete sacrifice;
> I give up myself, and whatever I know—
>   Now wash me, and I shall be whiter than snow.
> Lord Jesus, for this I most humbly entreat,
>   I wait, blessed Lord, at Thy crucified feet,
> By faith for my cleansing, I see thy blood flow—
>   Now wash me, and I shall be whiter than snow.
> *Refrain:*
> Whiter than snow, yes, whiter than snow,
>   Now wash me, and I shall be whiter than snow.[3]

---

3. Nicholson, "Whiter than Snow," First four verses and refrain, 1872 (public domain).

Day 39

Purged!

Purge me from every sinful blot: my idols all be cast aside.
Cleanse me from every evil thought, from all the filth of self and pride.
...
The hatred of my carnal mind out of my flesh at once remove;
Give me a tender heart, resigned, and pure, and fill'd with faith and love.
—Charles Wesley[1]

In the name of the First Amendment to the Constitution of the United States of America, which guarantees "freedom of speech" to its citizens, we have countless examples of content in print and cinema and on radio, television, and the internet that are offensive, destructive, and even dangerous to millions of people—not just in America but throughout the world. The garbage, especially that of a sexual nature, which we have spewed forth in the name of entertainment and freedom of speech has, quite understandably, grieved and angered countless people throughout world—including Muslim imams and their followers. It has caused the western world to suffer untold disrespect.

---

1. Wesley, "The Promise of Sanctification," Verses 7 & 10, "Christian Perfection," *The Works of the Rev. John Wesley: Forty-two sermons on various subjects*, 435.

39—Purged!

Especially since the advent of the internet and its widespread use, sinful thoughts can quickly be exacerbated and facilitated. By that I mean with the click of a mouse:

- An angry, marginalized person or a radical Islamic terrorist can indulge his or her desire for vengeance by learning how to build a bomb—and then do so, using it to wreak terror, destruction, and death.

- A jealous or greedy person bent on causing the death of another person in order to "get even" or become the benefactor of a large life insurance policy can learn how to commit the perfect crime—and then do so, leaving untold grief and disruption in its wake.

- A bitter, hate-filled person or a person involved in an illicit affair who wants to eliminate another person for his or her own satisfaction or personal agenda can learn how to hire a hit man—and then do so, leaving a tangled web of horror and loss.

- A depressed person feeling hopeless and helpless in the face of adverse circumstances can learn how to commit suicide—and then do so, turning the lives of friends and loved ones upside down and creating a wound that will never heal.

- A devious, dishonest person who is reluctant to pay all of his or her income taxes can learn how to cheat the government—and then do so, with the risk of ultimate exposure and even a jail sentence, to say nothing of making it more difficult for the government to provide needed services for others.

- A person struggling with sexual temptation can find a vast smorgasbord of erotic and pornographic pictures and videos to feed his fleshly desires in ways he never dreamed of and far beyond what he had in mind—and become embroiled in an embarrassing and destructive addiction that saps his time and energy and threatens his marriage and other relationships.

Examples could be multiplied, but you get the picture.

Along with the horror of such internet-driven scenarios, however, is good news of sorts. A person looking at websites containing the above-mentioned information can decide to abort the process; cease indulging his anger, jealousy, greed, bitterness, hatred, lust, or feelings of depression, hopelessness, and helplessness; and do something positive and constructive with his (or her) PC or Mac. He can hit the "Delete" key and/or, if there's a lengthy web-search history on the subject at hand, actually purge that history from his hard drive.

Think about it: if only King David had chosen to abort his lingering look at the unsuspecting Bathsheba taking a bath on her rooftop, he would never have invited her to the palace and seduced and/or violated her (2 Sam 11:1–27). She would never have become pregnant, let alone lost her child shortly after his birth. David would never have found it expedient to arrange for the murder of her husband Uriah. Uriah and Bathsheba could have enjoyed their marriage and had their own family. David would not have lost the respect of his own sons and his moral authority over them. And God would not have "raise[d] up evil" against him from his own family: rape, murder, rebellion, and treason.

If only David had pushed the "Delete" key at the moment the temptation presented itself! If only he had taken the "way out" (1 Cor 10:13), stopped looking, and occupied himself with something else! If only he had fled from the temptation, as Joseph did in Old Testament Egypt (Gen 39:7–14), and as Paul urged Timothy, his young son-in-the-faith, to do in the New Testament (2 Tim 2:22)!

Sadly, as history records, he *didn't*. But—after arranging for Uriah's murder, trying to cover the whole thing up, taking Bathsheba as his wife, and losing the child conceived through their illicit union—what *did* he do? After attempting to carry on, "business-as-usual," and hoping nobody had noticed, David was cleverly and boldly confronted by the prophet Nathan. After arousing David's ire through a fictitious, allegorical story, Nathan bluntly told him, "*You* are the man!" (2 Sam 12:1–12, italics mine).

Then what? How did David respond to that? He admitted what he'd done. He "said to Nathan, 'I have sinned against the LORD.' And Nathan said to David, 'The LORD also has taken away your sin; you shall not die'" (2 Sam 12:13). You've got to believe that David's confession was not some casual, bland, unemotional, Stoic statement of simple fact. Surely, it was a heartfelt, impassioned, emotional, shamefaced acknowledgement of the whole sordid affair. But notice what happened next: Nathan said, "The LORD also has taken away your sin."

That was huge! In spite of the multiple consequences of his gross disobedience to the commandments of the Lord (think commandments 3, 6, 7, and 10—for starters[2]), his sins were forgiven by the Lord; they were

2. See Exod 20.

deleted! The cloud of condemnation no longer hung over his head! The sin-induced separation (Isa 59:2) between him and his God was ended! His embarrassing and humiliating web-search history was purged! He was once again pure before the Lord!

The reason I know his confession was far deeper than his stark statement to Nathan might lead us to believe is that his actual acknowledgement of his sin and his heart-cry of appeal to the Lord are recorded in Psalm 51:

> Be gracious to me, O God, according to Your lovingkindness;
>> According to the greatness of Your compassion *blot out* my transgressions.
>
> *Wash* me thoroughly from my iniquity
>> And *cleanse* me from my sin.
>
> For I know my transgressions,
>> And my sin is ever before me.
>
> Against You, You only, I have sinned
>> And done what is evil in Your sight,
>
> So that You are justified when You speak
>> And blameless when You judge.
>
> Behold, I was brought forth in iniquity,
>> And in sin my mother conceived me.
>
> Behold, You desire truth in the innermost being,
>> And in the hidden part You will make me know wisdom.
>
> *Purify* me with hyssop, and I shall be *clean*;
>> *Wash* me, and I shall be *whiter than snow.*
>
> Make me to hear joy and gladness,
>> Let the bones which You have broken rejoice.
>
> Hide Your face from my sins
>> And *blot out* all my iniquities.
>
> Create in me a *clean* heart, O God,
>> And renew a steadfast spirit within me.
>
> Do not cast me away from Your presence
>> And do not take Your Holy Spirit from me.
>
> Restore to me the joy of Your salvation
>> And sustain me with a willing spirit.
>
> Then I will teach transgressors Your ways,
>> And sinners will be converted to You. . . .
>
> The sacrifices of God are a broken spirit;

> A broken and a contrite heart, O God, You will not despise
> (Ps 51:1–13, 17, italics mine).

David begged for his sins to be blotted out—*deleted*, and they were! He pled for his heart to be cleansed and purified—*purged*, and it was! No wonder he could then say:

> How blessed is he whose transgression is forgiven,
>   Whose sin is covered!
> How blessed is the man to whom the LORD does not impute iniquity,
>   And in whose spirit there is no deceit!
> When I kept silent about my sin, my body wasted away
>   Through my groaning all day long.
> For day and night Your hand was heavy upon me;
>   My vitality was drained away as with the fever heat of summer.
> I acknowledged my sin to You,
>   And my iniquity I did not hide;
> I said, "I will confess my transgressions to the LORD";
>   And You forgave the guilt of my sin (Ps 32:1–5).

My point in bringing all this up in a book on the Passion of Jesus Christ is that both the efficacy of the Old Covenant with its elaborate sacrificial system and the efficacy of the New Covenant with its life-changing gospel rest on it. All the bloody animal sacrifices of the Old Testament anticipated, prefigured, and climaxed in Jesus' bloody sacrifice of Himself. All the New Testament claims of remission, reconciliation, restoration, and regeneration harkened back to and reflected back on what happened on the cross. Remember: "without shedding of blood there is no forgiveness" (Heb 9:22b).

Perish the thought, but should you slip into a sin in thought, word, or deed, push the "Delete" key, cry out to God in confession and repentance, and receive fresh forgiveness through Jesus' shed blood. And if perchance you have a backlog of sin that you've heretofore failed to deal with, bring it all before the Lord, repent of it, appropriate His cleansing, and purge your "hard drive" of every "web-search." After all, Paul said that "our great God and Savior, Christ Jesus, . . . gave Himself for us to redeem us from every lawless deed, and to *purify* for Himself a people for His own possession, zealous for good deeds" (Titus 2:13b-14, italics mine).

39—Purged!

How relieved you'll feel as your conscience has been purged and your heart has been purified! In his impromptu sermon on the portico of Solomon at the Temple in Jerusalem, Peter urged his listeners to "... repent and return, so that your sins may be *wiped away [erased, purged]*, in order that times of refreshing may come from the presence of the Lord ..." (Acts 3:19, italics and brackets mine). Repent, and be refreshed!

Day 40

Reconciliation

As a follower of Jesus, I am called to work for justice and reconciliation, and to be an advocate for those who cannot speak for themselves. I plan to focus my future work on human rights and religious freedom—both domestic and international—as well as matters of the culture and the American family.

—Frank Wolf[1]

One enormous benefit of the atoning death of Jesus Christ on our behalf is reconciliation—the reconciliation of an estranged sinner to the holy God of the universe and the reconciliation of two human beings, groups, tribes, or even entire countries or societies that have been estranged from one another. The New Testament speaks pointedly about this. In Romans 5, Paul speaks to the "vertical" dimension: "For if while we were enemies we were reconciled to God through the death of His Son, much more, having been reconciled, we shall be saved by His life. And not only this, but we also exult in God through our Lord Jesus Christ, through whom we have now received the reconciliation" (vv. 10–11).

---

1. Quoted by Ben Pershing, "Frank Wolf to Retire after 17 Terms in Congress," *The Washington Post*, December 17, 2013. Frank Wolf is a former legislator who represented Virginia's 10th congressional district in the United States House of Representatives from January 1981 until his retirement in January 2015.

40—RECONCILIATION

In Colossians 1, Paul looks ahead to the end result of this magnificent "vertical" reconciliation: "And although you were formerly alienated and hostile in mind, engaged in evil deeds, yet He has now reconciled you in His fleshly body through death, in order to present you before Him holy and blameless and beyond reproach . . ." (vv. 21–22). Imagine that! At last: sinless perfection—when we've made the transition to glory at death or at His return! Not only that, but a couple of verses earlier, Paul explains, "For it was the Father's good pleasure for all the fullness to dwell in Him, and through Him to reconcile *all* things to Himself, having made peace through the blood of His cross; through Him, I say, whether things on earth or things in heaven" (vv. 19–20, italics mine). I don't pretend to know the full ramifications of that, but I'm certainly looking forward to finding out what they are when they all come to pass!

In 2 Corinthians 5, Paul speaks again to the "vertical" dimension: "Now all these things [the new things that come from being "in Christ," according to v. 17] are from God, who reconciled us to Himself through Christ . . . (vv. 18–19a, brackets mine). But in this chapter, he also introduces the "horizontal" dimension by saying that God "gave *us* the ministry of reconciliation, namely, that God was in Christ reconciling the world to Himself, not counting their trespasses against them, and He has committed to *us* the word of reconciliation" (v. 19b, italics mine). He concludes by saying, "Therefore, we are ambassadors for Christ, as though God were making an appeal through us; we beg you on behalf of Christ, be reconciled to God" (v. 20). Thus, we who have been reconciled to God through Christ are earnestly and passionately to share with others the message that they, too, can be reconciled to Him. That's called "evangelism"—presenting the gospel to those who have never heard or understood it.

But there's another aspect to this matter of "horizontal" reconciliation: that of human beings estranged from one another laying down their enmity toward each other, sincerely apologizing to each other, and forgiving each other. And that sort of thing happens most effectively when both parties have first experienced personal reconciliation with God and drawn inspiration from the example set by Christ. In the Sermon on the Mount, Jesus said this: "Therefore if you are presenting your offering at the altar, and there remember that your brother has something against you, leave your offering there before the altar and go; first be reconciled to your brother, and then come and present your offering" (Matt 5:23–24). In other words, if you've done something to hurt or offend a fellow-believer, you'd better apologize to him or her and seek his or her forgiveness before you try to participate in the worship of the triune God (including, by the way, an observance of The Lord's Supper).

But there's more! What Jesus did on the cross broke down barriers between whole *groups* or *ethnicities* of people, starting with Jews and Gentiles. Paul explains this remarkable phenomenon in Ephesians 2, where he addresses Gentiles who have put their faith in Jesus Christ:

> Therefore remember that formerly you, the Gentiles in the flesh, who are called "Uncircumcision" by the so-called "Circumcision," which is performed in the flesh by human hands—remember that you were at that time separate from Christ, excluded from the commonwealth of Israel, and strangers to the covenants of promise, having no hope and without God in the world. But now in Christ Jesus you who formerly were far off have been brought near by the blood of Christ. For He Himself is our peace, who made both groups into one and broke down the barrier of the dividing wall, by abolishing in His flesh the enmity, which is the Law of commandments contained in ordinances, so that in Himself He might make the two into one new man, thus establishing peace, and might reconcile them both in one body to God through the cross, by it having put to death the enmity" (vv. 11–16).

If only all the present-day Jews and Palestinians living in Israel understood and accepted this, because it's the only ultimate solution to the age-old enmity between them! If only all present-day African-Americans and white Americans understood and accepted this! If only all present-day American police officers and members of minority communities understood and accepted this! Such reconciliation would end the hatred, the hostility, the bitterness, the threats, the angry words, and the accusations—both true and false. It would end the attacks, the acts of violence, the murders, and the retaliation. It would usher in an era of peace and security.

I realize that a tiny minority of Jews and a small minority of Arabs who make their home in the Promised Land *do* embrace Jesus of Nazareth as their Messiah, and I realize that just before His return *all* Jews will, as will multitudes of Arabs. I realize that some members of our most troubled urban American communities and some members of the police departments that patrol them *do* embrace Jesus as their Savior and Lord, attempt to live out His teachings in their lives, and are part of the answer, not part of the problem, in their neighborhoods. But it will take the cataclysmic return of the Prince of Peace to bring about *total* reconciliation. Meanwhile, the only solution is for both sides to meet—and bow—at the cross. The common thread through all the Scriptures I've cited above is the cross, the death, and the blood of Christ.

In 1994, the Rwandan genocide—involving the Hutu and Tutsi tribes—nearly tore the country apart, killing nearly a million people. According to the evangelical-Christian, humanitarian organization known as World Vision, here's what happened:

> On the night of April 6, 1994, the plane carrying Rwandan President Juvenal Habyarimana, a Hutu, was shot down near the airport in Kigali, Rwanda's capital. It triggered a mass hysteria such as the world has rarely seen. In the next 100 days, nearly 20 percent of Rwanda's population would die—many by machete, blow by blow hacking away at peace, friendships, families, and communities.
>
> One of the many scenes of carnage was near [a man named] Andrew's village in Murambi. There 50,000 Tutsis were massacred in just eight hours in a vocational school where desperate families had taken refuge. Today, the site is preserved as a genocide memorial.
>
> The mass killing stopped when the Rwandan Patriotic Front, an army of Tutsis and moderate Hutus (led by current President Paul Kagame), seized the capital and took power in July 1994. In the aftermath, says Andrew, "hatred developed among people in this village. Those who survived against those who killed. Those friendships that characterized this village disappeared."
>
> [But] in 1996, when thousands of families began to return to their villages in Rwanda, World Vision started a reconciliation and peacebuilding department. "Reconciliation was necessary and a foundation for every initiative," says Josephine [Munyeli, World Vision's specialist for healing, peacebuilding, and reconciliation]. "If we were to do development work straightaway when people had not yet dealt with their painful past, we would be heading nowhere. People carrying deep pain cannot be productive."
>
> World Vision developed a reconciliation model that endures today: a two-week program of sharing intensely personal memories of the genocide, learning new tools to manage deeply painful emotions, and embarking on a path to forgiveness. The approach was replicated all over the country and embraced by the new government.
>
> "Thousands of people went through the process," says Josephine. "More than 200 trainers were trained. Two thousand survivors and perpetrators went through healing training. And 2,000

youth went through PRAY—Promotion of Reconciliation Among Youth—which used dance, drama, poetry, and artwork to help traumatized children express their feelings."[2]

There's much more to the story of the healing that has come about in Rwanda, but I'll mention just one example of the miraculous reconciliation that has taken place. Callixte, a childhood friend of Andrew, was a member of the mob that had killed Andrew's wife's entire family during the heat of the conflict. Needless to say, extreme animosity separated them. But now, thanks to the grace of God and His agents of reconciliation, Callixte (who, after being turned in to the authorities by Andrew, spent thirteen years in prison for his crimes) and Andrew are friends again, worship and serve in the same church, and "go to prisons together, visiting genocide perpetrators who are still incarcerated and talking with them about reconciliation. Learning to forgive has made all the difference for the two friends and their families. 'It has set us free, me and him,' says Andrew. 'It has set our families free.'"[3]

It seems to me that if individuals who have been either perpetrators or victims of such colossal atrocities can find a path to repentance, forgiveness, and reconciliation, we who have been estranged from others for what are probably much lesser offenses—often just sharp disagreements, perhaps even of a political nature—ought to be able to find that same path. We need to heed the words of St. Paul: "Never pay back evil for evil to anyone. Respect what is right in the sight of all men. If possible, so far as it depends on you, be at peace with all men" (Rom 12:17–18).

---

2. Kari Costanza, with contributions from Martin Tindiwensi *of World Vision in Rwanda*, "Rwanda: 20 Years Later," *World Vision Magazine*, May 2014, brackets mine.

3. Costanza, "Rwanda: 20 Years Later."

Day 41

Pearl Harbor and the God of Reconciliation

Yesterday, December 7, 1941—a date which will live in infamy—the United States of America was suddenly and deliberately attacked by naval and air forces of the Empire of Japan.

—President Franklin D. Roosevelt

True stories abound of former enemies who have been reconciled to one another through the cross of Christ—both individuals and groups, but one of the most remarkable comes from the bitter conflict between the Empire of Japan and the United States of America in the Pacific theater of World War II. It involves Mitsuo Fuchida, the most experienced pilot in the Japanese Navy, the aviator who led the shocking, surprise attack by Japan upon the United States Naval Base at Pearl Harbor, Hawaii; and Jacob "Jake" DeShazer, an American soldier who became a bombardier with the Jimmy Doolittle Squadron.

What happened on December 7, 1941, is long since a matter of horrific history. For three hours, 40 torpedo planes, 103 level bombers, 131 dive-bombers, and 79 fighters reigned terror on Pearl Harbor and nearby airfields, barracks, and dry docks.[1] Of the eight battleships in the harbor,

---

1. According to the National World War II Museum.

five were temporarily incapacitated. The Arizona was totally destroyed, and the Oklahoma, California, and West Virginia were sunk. The Nevada was beached and beginning to sink. Only the Pennsylvania, Maryland, and Tennessee could be repaired. The California, West Virginia, and Nevada were salvaged much later, but the Oklahoma, after being raised, was deemed worthless and re-sunk. Other smaller ships were damaged, as well, but the worst losses and damages were human ones. A total of 2,403 American military personnel and civilians were killed, and 1,178 were wounded.[2]

As a result of the atrocity, the United States declared war on Japan and entered a brutal and bloody conflict that lasted three years and eight months, took the lives of 11,606 American military personnel, 1,740,000 Japanese military personnel, and 393,400 Japanese civilians.[3] The enormous loss of civilian lives came largely through the devastation wreaked on Hiroshima and Nagasaki on the mornings of August 6 and August 9, 1945, when the United States dropped atomic bombs on those cities.

Those cataclysmic (and unprecedented) bombings finally brought about the surrender by Emperor Michinomiya Hirohito, representing Japan, to General Douglas MacArthur, representing the United States, on September 2, 1945,[4] and the war, at last, was officially over. The war's end also brought about the end of Mitsuo Fuchida's military career, since the Japanese forces were disbanded. He returned to his home village near Osaka and began farming, but he became increasingly frustrated and unhappy.

Meanwhile, motivated by a deep desire to take revenge on the Japanese for the sneak attack on Pearl Harbor, Jacob DeShazer an American soldier who had been on KP duty in an army camp in California when the news came over the radio, volunteered one month later for a secret mission with the Jimmy Doolittle Squadron—a surprise raid on Tokyo from the carrier Hornet. He was one of the bombardiers when they carried it out on April 18, 1942, but his elation over the raid soon turned to deep disappointment and then to violent hatred. As his plane flew toward China, it ran out of fuel, and the five crew members were forced to parachute into Japanese-held territory. The next morning DeShazer and the others were captured and became prisoners of war. During the ensuing forty long

---

2. According to the National World War II Museum.
3. According to the *Pacific War Online Encyclopedia.*
4. As chronicled in Bill O'Reilly's and Martin Dugard's book, *Killing the Rising Sun: How America Vanquished World War II Japan*, 259–62.

41—Pearl Harbor and the God of Reconciliation

months—twenty-four of them in solitary confinement, the unspeakably cruel treatment he received from his captors almost drove him insane.

After twenty-five months of confinement in Nanking, China, however, the US prisoners were given a Bible to read—just one. When it finally became DeShazer's turn to read it, he had three weeks to do so. As he pored over it, he came to realize that it was not just a historical classic of some sort, it was the word of God; and it became intensely relevant to him in his POW cell. Receiving Christ as his Lord and Savior on June 8, 1944, he experienced a dramatic change in his attitude toward his captors. His hatred turned into love and concern, and he resolved that, should his country win the war and he be liberated, he would someday return to Japan to introduce others to this life-changing book and the Christ he'd found through it.

His country did win the war, he was liberated, and after graduating from Seattle Pacific College, he did return to Japan as a missionary on December 28, 1948. The Emperor had publicly disavowed his divinity in 1946, so millions of Japanese were disillusioned—many even committing suicide—and searching for meaning in life. It's estimated that during DeShazer's first year as a missionary there were 30,000 conversions—as many as 10,000 during one ten-day campaign. Among them were many of DeShazer's former prison guards, including the one who had delivered the Bible to the prisoners in Nanking. DeShazer had recounted his story in pamphlet form and entitled it, "I Was a Prisoner of Japan," and the Bible Meditation League had printed a million copies of it for distribution throughout Japan.

One of the individuals who received a copy was Mitsuo Fuchida. As he got off the train one day in Tokyo's Shibuya Station, he saw an American distributing literature. When the American passed Fuchida, he gave him DeShazer's pamphlet. Since he was involved at the time with the trials pertaining to the atrocities committed against war prisoners, Fuchida put it in his pocket, intending to read it later. What he discovered, of course, was the account of DeShazer's confinement and conversion, and the message eventually changed his life. Since the American POW had found the message in the Bible, Fuchida decided to purchase one for himself—despite his Buddhist heritage.

During the following weeks, he read it eagerly. One day he came to the climactic scene: the crucifixion of Jesus of Nazareth. He read in Luke 23:34 the prayer Jesus prayed from the cross: "Father, forgive them, for they know not what they do." Fuchida was impressed that he was one of those for whom Jesus had prayed, for he had slaughtered so many men in the name of patriotism, thinking he was doing the right thing for his country and its emperor. He became a new person, and his whole outlook on life was changed. Soon the word of his conversion got out, and headlines appeared in newspapers: "Pearl Harbor Hero Converts to Christianity." Former war buddies came to visit him, attempting to persuade him to jettison "this crazy idea."

Instead he grew in his faith and became an evangelist, traveling across Japan and throughout the Orient to introduce others to Christ. He met DeShazer in person in 1950, and the two not only celebrated their brotherhood in Christ but later held evangelistic meetings together. On one occasion, they addressed a crowd of over 3,000 at a large hall in Osaka and saw large numbers come to Christ when they gave the invitation to do so. Fuchida died on May 30, 1976, and DeShazer attended his funeral in Japan.[5] DeShazer lived to be 95, dying on March 15, 2008.[6]

It's one of the strangest and most inspiring stories to come out of World War II: Mitsuo Fuchida, the Japanese pilot who bombed Pearl Harbor, and Jacob DeShazer, the Doolittle Raider who bombed Tokyo, became close friends and spiritual brothers. Bitter enemies grasped the love of God, repented, believed, were forgiven, and were reconciled to Him—and to one another—by the blood of Jesus Christ.

Is there someone to whom *you* need to be reconciled?

---

5. Jacob DeShazer, "Fuchida Remembered," *Japan Harvest*, Fall 1976, 18–19.

6. "Jacob Daniel DeShazer, 6584514, Staff Sergeant, Bombardier, Crew 16," Doolittle Tokyo Raiders.

Day 42

Monkey Business

You will find it is necessary to let things go,
simply for the reason that they are too heavy.

—Corrie ten Boom[1]

The writer of the Epistle to the Hebrews urged: ". . . let us also lay aside every encumbrance and the sin which so easily entangles us, and let us run with endurance the race that is set before us, fixing our eyes on Jesus, the author and perfecter of faith, who for the joy set before Him endured the cross, despising the shame, and has sat down at the right hand of the throne of God" (Heb 12:2). There's a reason why they call track stars and cross-country runners "thinclads": they don't wear heavy clothing; they don't wear steel-toed work boots; they don't carry an attaché case with them during the race. They could, but they choose not to. Why? Because they want to win the race—or at least finish it.

Many years ago, my youngest daughter ran in the Chicago Marathon—nearly 26½ miles. No, she didn't win; but she ran—or at least jogged—the whole race. She never walked; and she finished the course. She started the race with some sort of sweatshirt and plaid pajama bottoms over her tank top and running shorts, and she planned to shed those outer garments along the way. But it was a chilly day in Chicago, so she kept those on and

---

1. Debbie McDaniel, "40 Powerful Quotes from Corrie ten Boom."

felt quite comfortable. The point is: she didn't wear a long fur overcoat, she didn't wear combat boots, and she didn't carry a suitcase!

We too need to strip down . . . for the race of *life*. But often we don't want to let go of our pet sins, our pet indulgences, our pet idols, or our pet encumbrances that slow us down in the race of life. So, what's the answer? God Himself tells us. He says, "Cease striving"—or, "let go"—and know that I am God" (Ps 46:10). The Hebrew here translated "Cease striving" or "let go" probably means, "Stop!" "Strip down!" "Loosen your grip on everything else!" "Let go—and know!"

Yes, the answer is to choose, but it's to choose to let go, to let go and to know—to know that God is who and what He claims to be: the satisfier of our souls and the provider of every need. God has so much for us, if we'll just *let go!* Let go of what? Of everything that keeps us from following the Lord fully, from having a heart that is completely His, from really serving Him, from running the race successfully to the finish line, from worshiping and centering our lives around Him alone.

Jesus made it so plain. He said, "So then, none of you can be My disciple who does not give up [or, let go of] all his own possessions [the things he's clinging to, depending on, insisting on, giving himself to]" (Luke 14:33, brackets mine). He also said, "For whoever wishes to save his life will lose it; but whoever loses his life for My sake will find it" (Matt 16:25). Whoever goes the way of the cross and lets go of all that constitutes self-life here on planet Earth will find abundant and eternal life here and hereafter.

Stop and think about it: what or who could possibly be more important than knowing Jesus Christ and doing His will and serving Him??? Obviously, nothing and no one! And yet we let the devil lie to us and stress all the good times, pleasures, and fun we're going to miss if we let go of our sins, our worldliness, and our baggage. We allow him to obscure the issue.

But look at the perspective of Moses: "By faith Moses, when he had grown up, refused to be called the son of Pharaoh's daughter, choosing rather to endure ill-treatment with the people of God than to enjoy the passing pleasures of sin, considering the reproach of Christ greater riches than the treasures of Egypt; for he was looking to the reward. By faith he left Egypt, not fearing the wrath of the king; for he endured, as seeing Him who is unseen" (Heb 11:24–27). He went "the way of the cross" centuries before anyone had invented death by crucifixion, let alone infused it with the meaning that sprang from Jesus' death on that barbaric instrument of execution.

And listen to the perspective of Paul: "More than that, I count all things to be loss in view of the surpassing value of knowing Christ Jesus my Lord, for whom I have suffered the loss of all things, and count them but rubbish so that I may gain Christ . . ." (Phil 3:8). Keep in mind the fact that Paul had let go of his status, his reputation, his self-righteousness, his anger, his hatred, his ethnic pride, his religious pedigree, and his misguided zeal for persecuting the church of Jesus Christ when he came to know the true and living God.

Somewhere in Africa or India, I'm told, hunters have an interesting method of catching monkeys. It's simple, but it's very effective. In a clearing in the forest or the jungle, they place a hollowed-out gourd with a treat in it—perhaps candy of some sort. They use a gourd with an opening just big enough for a monkey's little hand to slip in but just small enough to keep his hand from coming out again if he has made a fist. All the monkey has to do to go free is let go of the candy, but he won't; thus, he is trapped, because as he drags the gourd around, he's weighted down, and he's easily caught.

If you're still hanging onto, grasping, clutching, insisting on keeping or continuing in something that you know displeases God and has you in bondage, what is it that Jesus is saying to you today? He's saying, "One thing you still lack; sell all you possess." "Let go . . . and know that I am God." "Experience My love, My power, My goodness, My deliverance, My reality." Are you ready to do that? Are you ready to let go of the sins and the baggage in your life that are keeping you from a 100-percent commitment to the Lord Jesus? Are you willing to release your clutch on the candy in your life and pray as missionary Jim Elliot, who was martyred in Ecuador in 1956 by the Stone Age Auca (Huaorani) Indians, did in July 1948? Here's what he wrote in his journal:

> Father, let me be weak that I might loose[2] my clutch on everything temporal. My life, my reputation, my possessions, Lord, let me loose the tension of the grasping hand. Even, Father, would I lose the love of fondling. How often I have released a grasp only to retain what I prized by "harmless" longing, the fondling touch. Rather open my hand to receive the nail of Calvary, as Christ's was opened—that I, releasing all, might be released from all that binds

---

2. This is not a typo, nor is the same word in the next sentence. In both cases, Jim *meant* to use the word "loose," not the word "lose." In the following sentence, however, he did use the word "lose."

me now. He thought Heaven, yea, equality with God, not a thing to be clutched at. So let me release my grasp."[3]

It's a very sensible exchange. As Jim said elsewhere, "He is no fool who gives what he cannot keep to gain what he cannot lose."[4]

---

3. Elizabeth Elliot, *Shadow of the Almighty*, 1958, 59.
4. Elliot, *Shadow*, 108.

Day 43

MONEY BUSINESS

Abundance isn't God's provision for me to live in luxury.
It's his provision for me to help others live.
God entrusts me with his money not to build my kingdom on Earth,
but to build his Kingdom in Heaven.

—RANDY ALCORN[1]

SURVEYS SHOW THAT THE vast majority of today's evangelical Christians fail to give anything resembling the biblically normative tithe (10 percent) of their income to the work of the Lord. As Eric Metaxas has pointed out in a *Breakpoint* commentary on September 20, 2018,

> ... in this time of material abundance, a lot of worthy churches and ministries face a chronic shortage of funds. Why is that? According to nonprofitsource.com,[2] Christians today give only 2.5 percent of their income; during the Great Depression, it was 3.3 percent. The average giving by adults who attend Protestant churches in America is about $17 a week, and 37 percent of regular church attendees and evangelicals don't give *any* money to church.[3]

---

1. Alcorn, *Money, Possessions, and Eternity*, 133.
2. "Online Giving for Churches," under "Charitable Giving Statistics," *The Ultimate List of Online Giving Statistics for 2017*.
3. Metaxas, "Christian Hoarding?" *Breakpoint Daily*, September 20, 2018.

Although I could certainly do so, I'm not interested today in launching a defense of my view that giving 10 percent of one's income to one's local church and giving above that to special appeals within and outside of one's local church—especially to the cause of global evangelization or world missions—ought to be the norm. But because I *believe* that (and have both practiced and promoted it for over fifty years), I *am* interested in pointing out the disappointing lack of basic stewardship and generosity among those claiming to be God's people—Christ-followers. I could speculate in depth about the reasons for that, but I will suggest only two.

The first is that too many preachers (especially televangelists) have said *too much* about money, both shaming and manipulating people into giving (usually to them and their pet causes), making biblically indefensible promises, and leaving a trail of disillusioned donors, who feel used and abused. The second is that too many preachers (especially pastors), fearful of turning parishioners and visitors off, have said *too little* about money, leaving church members and attendees in the dark about biblical stewardship, about habitual and faithful giving, about investing in the greatest enterprise in human history, and about reaping eternal rewards—laying up treasures in heaven.

Understandably, you may be wondering what all this has to do with a book on prizing the Passion of our Lord. Please allow me to explain. Our giving, according to the book I call the "Maker's Manual,"[4] should be a response to the gracious generosity of the Giver of every good and perfect gift (Jas 1:17), to the poignant relinquishment of the One who gave His own unique and beloved Son up to the cross to purchase our redemption (Rom 8:3), and to the outrageous magnanimity of the One who offers us eternal life as a free gift through Him (Rom 6:23b).

Reflecting this attitude of heart, Paul talks freely and unashamedly about money in his second letter to the church at Corinth, Greece. Roger Barrier beautifully explains:

> Paul was collecting an offering for the brothers and sisters. The Corinthians didn't do a very good job with the offering. They started well with their giving, but then quit. Paul is encouraging

---

4. For well over twenty-six and a half years, Randy Shaffer, my broadcast engineer, and I produced a weekly, Sunday-morning radio program by that title. It aired for a while on three stations, located in three different south-central Pennsylvania counties, but for all those years it was a fixture on a secular AM station in York County (WSBA), and for most of those years it was also a fixture on a contemporary-Christian-music FM station in Lancaster County (WJTL).

43 — Money Business

them to finish out their commitment. He used the Macedonians as the motivation for his pep talk.

> *"And now, brothers, we want you to know about the grace that God has given the Macedonian churches. Out of the most severe trial, their overflowing joy and their extreme poverty welled up in rich generosity. And they did not do as we expected, but they gave themselves first to the Lord . . ."* (2 Cor 8:1-4, NIV).

The Macedonians experienced the grace of giving as they watched Jesus climb down the ladder. *"For you know the grace of our Lord Jesus Christ, that though he was rich, yet for your sakes he became poor, so that you through his poverty might become rich"* (2 Cor 8:9, NIV).

Think of the richness of Christ: The whole universe was His. He had only to speak one word and a new world would be created. He could put His finger on every star and say, "Mine!" Angels did his bidding. He was God.

Yet he became poor. Can you see Him stripping Himself of His glory as described in Philippians 2? Described by the "kenosis,"[5] he emptied Himself of His glory and Godness [vv. 5-8].

See Him in a dirty stable.

See Jesus, who dug the ocean beds, saying to a woman, "Give me a drink."

He saw the foxes and the birds going back to their nests and He had to say, "Foxes have holes, birds have nests; but, I have nowhere to lay My head."

Once He was honored by the "Hallelujahs!" of heaven, and now He is spat upon, struck, and cursed. The very hands that he had made were held still while the creature hammered stakes through the Creator's hands.

He was put upon a cross to bleed and die. He suffered the burden of the sin of the entire world. This is how the Macedonians gave so much. They looked down the ladder at Jesus and they saw Him with the people at the bottom.[6]

---

5. The theological term "kenosis" derives from the Greek word *ekenosen*, which is translated "emptied" in Phil 2:6-7, where Paul, referencing Jesus, says that ". . . although He existed in the form of God, [He] did not regard equality with God a thing to be grasped, but *emptied* Himself, taking the form of a bond-servant, and being made in the likeness of men . . ." (brackets and italics mine). In other words, He stripped Himself of the independent use of His divine attributes in order to walk among us as a human being and ultimately to lay down His life for us on a Roman cross.

6. Barrier, "Why Are Christians So Miserable at Giving?" *Crosswalk.com*, December 7, 2015, brackets mine.

They saw what Isaac Watts centuries later would say so accurately in song: "Love so amazing, so divine, demands my soul, my life, my all."[7] They responded as would Frances Ridley Havergal still later in song: "Take my silver and my gold, not a mite would I withhold."[8] How's *your* stewardship of the resources with which God has entrusted you?

---

7. Watts, "When I Survey the Wondrous Cross," Verse 4, 1707 (public domain).
8. Havergal, "Take My Life and Let It Be," Verse 4 (first half), 1874 (public domain).

Day 44

THEORIES OF THE ATONEMENT (PART 1)

We are told that Christ was killed for us, that His death has washed out our sins, and that by dying He disabled death itself. That is the formula. That is Christianity. That is what has to be believed. Any theories we build up as to how Christ's death did all this are, in my view, quite secondary: mere plans or diagrams to be left alone if they do not help us, and, even if they do help us, not to be confused with the thing itself. All the same, some of these theories are worth looking at.

—C.S. Lewis[1]

DOWN THROUGH THE CENTURIES of church history, theologians of all stripes have wrestled with the meaning of the Atonement of Jesus Christ for the sins of mankind. Based largely on different terms used by the writers of Scripture to describe the Atonement and its effect on the sinner who accepts it, they have come up with several "theories" to explain and understand it. At the risk of gross oversimplification and with the help primarily of the insights of two outstanding theologians, Gordon Lewis (one of my

---

1. Lewis, *Mere Christianity*, 58–9.

beloved mentors) and Bruce Demarest,[2] I'll list and try to explain some of them for you.

First, there's the *ransom* theory, which focuses on Jesus' deliverance of repentant sinners from enslaving powers, perhaps even paying a ransom to Satan to buy them back from his dominion over them—like the buying-back of a hostage from a kidnapper. At first glance, that may sound a bit strange, but Jesus *had* told His twelve original disciples that "the Son of Man did not come to be served, but to serve, and to give His life a *ransom for many*" (Mark 10:45, italics mine); and He *had* told His Jewish contemporaries, "You are of your father, the devil" (John 8:44).

Not only that, but Paul referred to Satan as "the god of this world" (2 Cor 4:4), and John said that "the whole world lies in the power of the evil one" (1 John 5:19). Paul explained that before our spiritual conversions we were "dead in [our] trespasses and sins, in which [we] formerly walked according to the course of this world, according to the prince of the power of the air, of the spirit that is now working in the sons of disobedience" (Eph 2:1–2). Besides, Paul made it clear to all Christ-followers that our bodies are now temples of the Holy Spirit, that we're not our own, and that we've "been bought with a price" (1 Cor 6:19–20). So, it's more than a theory: if you've been born of the Holy Spirit into the family of God, you've been ransomed—paid for—by the Son of Man, Jesus, the Christ.

Second, there's the *penal substitution* theory, which views the Atonement as a judicial punishment for man's sin suffered by Christ vicariously in man's place. The idea is that through His bloody death we, who in repentance and faith embrace that offer of pardon, don't have to experience the just punishment for our sinful rebellion against the Creator-God of the universe: the wrath of God—eternal separation from Him in hell (Matt 10:28), *gehenna*, the lake of fire, the garbage dump of the universe, prepared initially for the devil and his host of fallen angels (Matt 25:41).[3]

Scriptures, some already cited in this volume, come flooding to mind. John the Baptist said, "He who believes in the Son has eternal life; but he who does not obey the Son will not see life, but the wrath of God abides on him" (John 3:36). Paul explained, "Much more then, having now been justified by His blood, we shall be saved from the wrath of God through

---

2. Lewis and Demarest, "Christ's Once-for-All Atoning Provisions," *Integrative Theology*, Volume Two, Chapter 7, 372–8.

3. Jesus, to the surprise of many of our contemporaries, actually said more about hell than anyone else in Scripture.

44—Theories of the Atonement (Part 1)

Him" (Rom 5:9). Peter asserted: ". . . Christ also suffered for you . . . He Himself bore our sins in His body on the cross . . ." (1 Pet 2:21, 24). As long as we don't limit the intent of His atonement only to "the elect"—since John made it clear that "He Himself is the propitiation for our sins; and not for ours only, but also for those of the whole world" (1 John 2:2), you and I can certainly resonate with this theory, because Jesus has indeed been our Substitute (as we saw clearly on Day 2). Indeed, substitutionary atonement is the predominant explanation for the Passion of the Christ in the New Testament.

Third, there's the *moral influence* theory, which suggests that the love of Jesus—demonstrated so graphically through His suffering and death on the cross—impacts sinners so powerfully that, in countless cases, they drop their hostility toward God, repent of their sins, and are reconciled to Him. Even though this view is held primarily by liberal theologians, not evangelicals, there's a certain amount of truth to it.

Peter told his readers throughout the Roman Empire, ". . . you have been called for this purpose, since Christ also suffered for you, leaving you *an example* for you to follow in His steps, WHO COMMITTED NO SIN, NOR WAS ANY DECEIT FOUND IN HIS MOUTH; and while being reviled, He did not revile in return; while suffering, He uttered no threats, but kept entrusting Himself to Him who judges righteously . . ." (1 Pet 2:21–23, italics mine). Perhaps *you* have been won to faith in Christ by the exemplary love He displayed on the cross.

Fourth, there's the *satisfaction* theory, which sees the Atonement as satisfying the wounded honor of God, as compensating for the damages and dishonor done to the holy God of the universe by our sinful rebellion against him. It sees only Jesus Christ—who was (and is) God in the flesh and the only human being ever to live a life totally free from sin—as capable of providing this satisfaction.

Surely there's at least a measure of truth to this theory, in that the Holy Spirit revealed the following to Isaiah the prophet (some seven-hundred years before Jesus' birth on earth): "As a result of the anguish of His [the Messiah's] soul, He [God the Father] will see it and be *satisfied*; by His knowledge the Righteous One, My [the Father's] Servant, will justify the many, as He [the Messiah] will bear their iniquities" (Isa 53:11, brackets and italics mine). It's certainly true that you and I need to see our sins—our rebellious attempts at autonomy—as having deeply offended and wounded the heart of the God who had nothing but our best interests at heart in giving us His commandments, His guidelines, and His principles for life.

Fifth, there's the *government* theory, which sees the Atonement as necessary to restore the moral order of the universe. It sees the sufferings of Christ as maintaining the honor of the divine Ruler, revealing the ugliness of our sin, foreshadowing the eternal punishment of those who fail to repent, and actually restraining sin by striking fear into our hearts. Although its advocates wrongly fail to see Jesus' sacrifice as paying the penalty for our sins, they see it, oddly, as a substitute *for* penalty, one that provides a moral basis for divine forgiveness without compromising either God's holiness or the integrity of moral government.

Again, there's an element of truth in this theory, in that the moral order of the universe was certainly disrupted by the Fall of man in the Garden of Eden (Gen 3), is potentially restored through Jesus' death on the cross (Rom 3:21–26), and will only be completely restored by His return and the literal, visible establishment of His kingship over the entire universe (Rom 8:16–23; Rev 21:1–8). For you and me, Jesus' atonement has indeed made it possible for God to be "just *and* the justifier of the one who has faith in Jesus" (Rom 3:26, italics mine).

Sixth, there's the *reconciliation* theory, which suggests that Christ's death objectively reconciles the entire world to God. Postulated by neo-orthodox theologian Karl Barth, it rejects the idea that by His suffering Christ propitiated the wrath of the offended God. Instead it suggests that God's wrath fell both on Him *and* on us in solidarity with Him. Further, it sees the entire world as having been won back to the Father but admits that not everyone knows this. Thus, the work of the Holy Spirit (and, one would assume, Christ-followers) is to awaken this awareness of reconciliation in the hearts of all human beings.

This theory hints, therefore, at universalism—the view that ultimately everyone will be saved; and numerous Scriptures teach just the opposite. As confused and confusing as this theory is, we can agree at least with its emphasis on reconciliation—for reasons made clear, hopefully, on Days 40 and 41. Surely Jesus' death on the cross opens the door for reconciliation with God and reconciliation with one another in the human race—but only for those who grasp something of the gravity of their sin and its consequences, repent of it, cry out for forgiveness, and embrace the Atonement for themselves.

44—Theories of the Atonement (Part 1)

There's yet another theory, but that will have to wait until our next time together. Meanwhile, hopefully, the very fact that there *are* several theories—that the entire meaning of the Atonement cannot be contained in just one—will impress you with its breadth and depth.

Day 45

THEORIES OF THE ATONEMENT (PART 2)

Beware of the pleasant view of the Fatherhood of God—
God is so kind and loving that of course He will forgive us.
That sentiment has no place whatever in the New Testament.
The only ground on which God can forgive us is
the tremendous tragedy of the Cross of Christ;
to put forgiveness on any other ground is unconscious blasphemy.
—OSWALD CHAMBERS[1]

THUS FAR, WE'VE IDENTIFIED six theories advanced historically to help us grasp the rationale behind the Atonement:

- The ransom theory,
- The penal substitution theory,
- The moral influence theory,
- The satisfaction theory,
- The government theory, and
- The reconciliation theory.

1. Chambers, *My Utmost for His Highest*, 325.

45—Theories of the Atonement (Part 2)

But there's yet another: the *Christus Victor* theory, which—though originally postulated by the Orthodox Church centuries ago—has gained a significant measure of popularity among trendy evangelicals in recent years. It rightly emphasizes, as Mark Galli explains, that "Christ is victor. Christ in his death and resurrection overcame . . . the hostile powers that hold humanity in subjection, those powers variously understood as the devil, sin, the law, and death."[2] Indeed, Paul says clearly (and note the context of real moral guilt, spiritual hopelessness, and divine forgiveness):

> When you were dead in your transgressions and the uncircumcision of your flesh, He made you alive together with Him, having forgiven us all our transgressions, having canceled out the certificate of debt consisting of decrees against us, which was hostile to us; and He has taken it out of the way, having nailed it to the cross. When He had disarmed the rulers and authorities [Satan and his host of demons], He made a public display of them, having triumphed over them through Him" (Col 3:13–15, brackets mine).

Thus, the proponents of this theory are right: there's a cosmic dimension to the effects of Jesus' atoning death on the cross; it dealt a massive blow to the dark side of the spirit world. Not only that, but in a real sense we're trapped in our sin and need to be rescued, as suggested in Hebrews 2:14–15. But, as Mark Galli points out, "the theory's anthropology (view of humanity) emphasizes not our guilt but our victimhood, at least the way it is often discussed today."[3]

That, of course, fits nicely with the massive ownership of victimhood (as opposed to personal responsibility) in contemporary American culture; and perhaps that accounts for its rising popularity. It's not our job, however, to adjust our theology to fit current cultural trends. Besides, as Galli says, "Add to this the extensive discussion of substitutionary atonement in Romans, Galatians, and Hebrews—and *no* extensive discussions of Christus Victor anywhere in the New Testament—and one begins to wonder how much stock we should put in Christus Victor."[4] Not enough, surely, to minimize, contradict, ridicule, or reject the Bible-based, time-honored theory of the vicarious, substitutionary atonement. I agree with Mark Galli,

---

2. Galli, "The Problem with Christus Victor," *Christianity Today*, April, 2011. Galli, then the Managing Editor of *Christianity Today*, is now its Editor in Chief.

3. Galli, "The Problem."

4. Galli, "The Problem."

who concludes, "In my view, more than ever in our day, we need Christus Vicarious."⁵

Sadly, there is at least one contemporary pastor and would-be-theologian that rejects *all* traditional theories of the Atonement, grossly misrepresenting them, and suggesting, for example, that some "portray the Father of Jesus as a pagan deity who can only be placated by the barbarism of child sacrifice"!⁶ No, they don't! They portray Him as He is: the holy, omnipotent, omnipresent, omniscient, compassionate, gracious, and merciful God of the universe who devised—in eternity past—a way for His rebellious creatures to be forgiven and reconciled to Him, and that way is through the unjust, bloody, barbaric suffering and death of His beloved Son!

In his bizarre blog, this misguided pastor insists that "we don't mean that God required the vicious murder of His Son in order to forgive."⁷ Oh, yes, we do—although we wouldn't choose to word it quite like that! There is no other basis for forgiveness! Remember the blunt statement of the writer of the Epistle to the Hebrews as he reflected on the whole sacrificial system under the Old Covenant and saw its fulfillment in the death of the Lamb of God under the New Covenant: "without shedding of blood there is no forgiveness" (Heb 9:22)! And please review the quotation by Oswald Chambers under the title of today's commentary.

Perhaps we need to remind this angry blogger that, as we saw on Day 6, ". . . this Man [Jesus of Nazareth was] delivered over [to the cross] by the predetermined plan and foreknowledge of *God*" (Acts 2:23, brackets and italics mine). Perhaps we need to remind him that the Father "did not spare His own Son, but delivered Him over [to the cross] for us all" (Rom 8:32). Perhaps we need to remind him that ". . . the Lord [God the Father] was *pleased* to crush Him [the Messiah—Jesus, as it turned out], putting Him to grief; if He would render Himself as a guilt offering, He will see His [spiritual] offspring, He will prolong His days [rise from the dead], and the good pleasure of the Lord will prosper in His hand (Isa 53:10, italics and brackets mine).

By that, the prophet—clearly writing under the inspiration of the Holy Spirit—does not mean, surely, that God is some sort of sadist who *enjoyed* the ghastly death of His Son but rather that He was pleased with His beloved Son's obedience to the ultimate purpose of His visit to this planet

---

5. Galli, "The Problem," italics mine.
6. Brian Zhand, "How Does 'Dying for Our Sins' Work?" April 16, 2014, 1.
7. Zhand, "How Does," 2.

45—Theories of the Atonement (Part 2)

and that He was pleased with what His Passion accomplished on behalf of sinful human beings (as stressed on Day 3). I urge you to read and meditate on the entire fifty-third chapter of Isaiah to get a fuller picture of what the Atonement meant to God the Father, cost God the Son, and *should* mean for us wayward, needy sheep.

According to a reasonably reliable report, Karl Barth, the aforementioned neo-orthodox theologian,

> . . . was fielding questions from the audience after a lecture in Rockefeller Chapel on the campus of the University of Chicago in 1962. A student stood and asked him if he could summarize his life's work in theology in one sentence. According to the story, a gasp went up from the audience—responding to the student's perceived audaciousness. Also, according to the story, Barth didn't skip a beat. He said (paraphrasing), "Yes. In the words of a song I learned at my mother's knee: 'Jesus loves me, this I know, for the Bible tells me so.'"[8]

That, of course, is the beginning of a beloved song sung in Sunday Schools all over the United States and around the world—including mine as I was growing up in Oak Park, Illinois. I realize that the orthodox, evangelical view of the Bible (that, in its entirety, it is the objective, Spirit-breathed, inerrant word of God) differs significantly from Barth's view of it (that it simply points us to Christ; that it is not, per se, the word of God; and that it becomes the word of God to an individual only as he (or she) subjectively perceives *as the word of God* whatever portion of the Bible speaks to him or impresses him at a given moment).

But there's something refreshing about the simplicity of Barth's answer. And you can take it to the bank: Jesus *does* love you! How can you *know* that? He proved it when He died on the cross *for* you (Rom. 5:8)! How can you know *that*? The *Bible* tells you so!

---

8. Roger E. Olson, "Karl Barth's 'Jesus Loves Me, This I Know . . .' Answer: Can Anyone Verify It?" *Patheos: Hosting the Conversation on Faith*, Gordon-Conwell Theological Seminary, December 23, 2012.

Day 46

Conclusion

*We may not always hear God perfectly,
either in prayer or in our study of Scripture,
but if we know what he is like enough to love him
the way he is, he has ways to work out
our imperfections in hearing him.
When we perceive and reflect his heart,
especially the love that nailed Jesus to the cross,
we can best say, we "know God" (1 John 4:7–12).*

—Craig S. Keener[1]

Hopefully, these forty-six meditations (including this, the Conclusion) on the Passion of our Lord have helped to prepare you for the climactic days of Holy Week—for Maundy Thursday, Good Friday, Holy Saturday, and Easter Sunday. Hopefully, better yet, they have helped to prepare you for life—for the kind of life Jesus has called you to live. Hopefully, still better, they have helped to prepare you for death—for a daily death to self, sin, Satan, and the world-system.

Hopefully, best of all, they have helped to prepare you for eternity—for heaven, where you will fall down before the Lamb and sing a new song,

---

1. Keener, *Gift & Giver: The Holy Spirit for Today*, 17.

saying, "Worthy are You to take the book and to break its seals; for You were slain, and purchased for God with Your blood men from every tribe and tongue and people and nation. You have made them to be a kingdom and priests to our God; and they will reign upon the earth" (Rev 5:9–10).

Although Jesus is, to be sure, "the *Lion* that is from the tribe of Judah" (Rev 5:5, italics mine), He's also "a *Lamb*, standing, as if slain" (Rev 5:6, italics mine). You may remember that when Jesus appeared to His disciples on Easter Sunday night, "He showed them His hands and His feet" (Luke 24:40). Forty days later, just before—and as—He began His ascent back to heaven from the Mount of Olives, "He lifted up His hands and blessed them" (Luke 24:50). As Gerard Kelly, the former Senior Pastor of Crossroads International Church in Amsterdam, Holland, has pointed out, "The last image the disciples have of their Messiah, the suffering servant, is of his wounded, risen, glorified hands."[2]

We too will see Him throughout eternity as a Lamb that has been wounded and slain, as the One who has shed His own blood for our sins. We'll see the nail prints in His wrists and feet and the spear-caused puncture in His side—healed, of course, but still visible—to remind us of the price He paid for our redemption. Forever and ever we'll love Him, serve Him, and worship Him for who He is and for what He's done. Forever we'll prize His Passion.

And we'll never tire in doing so, because we'll be there in our new, glorified, resurrection bodies with our new, glorified, resurrection voices. Those of us who had "obsolete pitch" in this life will have absolute (perfect) pitch in the life to come! Those Christ-followers who are now deaf will hear the roar of worship by the innumerable company of saints and angels (Rev 6:11–14)! Those believers who are now physically blind will have perfect sight (1 John 3:2)!

You may have heard of Fanny Crosby, the blind American poet and songwriter, who cherished the fact that the first face she'd ever see *anywhere* would be that of Jesus, once she was absent from her earthly body and present with Him in heaven. Here are the first verse and chorus of her poignant song, "My Savior First of All":

> When my life work is ended, and I cross the swelling tide,
> > When the bright and glorious morning I shall see,
> I shall know my Redeemer when I reach the other side,

---

2. Kelly, *Encounter with God*, Oct/Nov/Dec 2010, 64.

>   And His smile will be the first to welcome me.
>   I shall know Him, I shall know Him,
>   And redeemed by His side, I shall stand.
>   I shall know Him, I shall know Him,
>   By the print of the nails in His hand.[3]

And so will you and I. I hope to see you on the other side!

---

[3]. Crosby, "My Savior First of All," First verse and chorus, 1894 (public domain). Crosby lived from 1820 to 1915. Her 8,000+ hymns and gospel songs are all now public domain.

Benediction

Now the God of peace,
who brought up from the dead
the great Shepherd of the sheep
through the blood of the eternal covenant,
even Jesus our Lord,
equip you in every good thing to do His will,
working in us that which is pleasing in His sight,
through Jesus Christ,
to whom be the glory forever and ever.
Amen.
—Hebrews 13:20—21

Bibliography

Alcorn, Randy. *Money, Possessions, and Eternity.* Carol Stream, IL: Tyndale House, 2003 (revised and updated version of book originally copyrighted in 1989 by Eternal Perspective Ministries).

Amplified Bible, The. Grand Rapids, MI: Zondervan, 1991.

Augsburger, Myron S. "The Cross and Forgiveness." *Two Sermons by Myron S. Augsburger.* Great Sermon Series, W-6103-LP. Waco, TX: Word Records, no date.

Barnard, Fiona. *Encounter with God.* Valley Forge, PA: Scripture Union, Jul/Aug/Sep 2016.

Barnes, Albert. *Barnes' Notes on the New Testament.* Grand Rapids, MI: Kregel, 1962.

Barrier, Roger. "Why Are Christians So Miserable at Giving?" *Crosswalk.com*, December 7, 2015. http://www.crosswalk.com/church/giving/why-are-christians-so-miserable-at-giving.html.

Bernard of Clairvaux (1091–1153). "O Sacred Head, Now Wounded," translated by James W. Alexander, 1829 (public domain). *Great Hymns of the Faith* (compiled and edited by John W. Peterson). Grand Rapids, MI: Singspiration Music, Zondervan, Twentieth printing, 1974, #116.

Bliss, Philip. "Hallelujah! What a Savior!" 1875 (public domain). *Great Hymns of the Faith* (compiled and edited by John W. Peterson). Grand Rapids, MI: Singspiration Music, Zondervan, Twentieth printing, 1974, #127.

Bonhoeffer, Dietrich. *Dietrich Bonhoeffer: Writings Selected with an Introduction by Robert Coles. Modern Spiritual Masters Series.* Maryknoll, NY: Orbis, 1998.

———. *The Cost of Discipleship.* Originally published in 1937. Translated from the German by R. H. Fuller and Irmgard Booth in 1949. Second Edition. New York, NY: MacMillan, 1959.

Buechner, Frederick. *The Faces of Jesus: A Life Story.* Brewster, MA: Paraclete, 2006.

Chambers, Oswald. *My Utmost for His Highest.* New York, NY: Dodd, Mead & Company, 1962 (34th printing of volume originally published in 1935).

Cocteau, Jean. *Le Rappel à L'Ordre.* Paris, France: Librairie Stock, 1926.

Cogdill, Roy E. "The Trial of Jesus." *Truth Magazine,* Guardian of Truth XXXI:20 (October 15, 1987).

Colson, Charles. *The Body.* Dallas, TX: Word, 1992.

———. "The Context of Forgiveness: Grace in Amish Country." *Breakpoint.* October 3, 2007.

———. "Who Killed Jesus? Setting the Record Straight." *Breakpoint.* February 12, 2004.

———. "Why U.S. Soldiers Donate Blood to Injured Terrorists." *Breakpoint.* March 6, 2007.

Bibliography

Cook, Steven R. *The Cross of Christ: Sufficient to Save.* Charleston, SC: CreateSpace, 2013.

Cooke, Gordon. "Look Both Ways." *Encounter with God.* Valley Forge, PA: Scripture Union, July/Aug/Sep 2018.

Costanza, Kari. "Rwanda: 20 Years Later." *World Vision Magazine*, May 2014. http://rwanda.worldvision magazine.org/#!introduction.

Cowper, William. "There Is a Fountain Filled with Blood," 1772 (public domain). *Great Hymns of the Faith* (compiled and edited by John W. Peterson). Grand Rapids, MI: Singspiration Music, Zondervan, Twentieth printing, 1974, #222.

Crosby, Fanny. "My Savior First of All," 1894 (public domain). *Great Hymns of the Faith* (compiled and edited by John W. Peterson). Grand Rapids, MI: Singspiration Music, Zondervan, Twentieth printing, 1974, #502.

Cymbala, Jim. *The Church God Blesses.* Grand Rapids, MI: Zondervan, 2002.

DeShazer, Jacob. "Fuchida Remembered." *Japan Harvest*, Fall 1976.

Dorsett, Lyle Wesley. *E. M. Bounds: Man of Prayer.* Grand Rapids, MI: Zondervan, 1991.

Downs, Ray. "Britain appoints Minister of Loneliness to tackle health problem 'worse than smoking.'" https://www.upi.com/Top_News/World-News/2018/01/17/Britain-appoints-Minister-of-Loneliness-to-tackle-health-problem-worse-than-smoking/7621516247564/.

Doyle, Larry. "Pathologist Examines Jesus' Death." *The York Dispatch*. March 22, 1986.

Duewel, Wesley. *Touch the World through Prayer.* Grand Rapids, MI: Zondervan, 1986.

Elliot, Elizabeth. *Shadow of the Almighty.* San Francisco, CA: Harper & Row, 1958; first paperback edition published in 1979.

———. *Through Gates of Splendor.* Ada, MI: Baker, 1975.

English Standard Version, The. Wheaton, IL: Crossway Bibles, Good News, 2011.

Fieldsend, John. *Encounter with God.* Valley Forge, PA: Scripture Union, Jul/Aug/Sep 2006.

Fu, Bob. *God's Double Agent: The True Story of a Chinese Christian's Fight for Freedom.* Grand Rapids, MI: Baker, 2013.

Gabriel, Charles H. "He Lifted Me," 1905 (public domain). *Great Hymns of the Faith* (compiled and edited by John W. Peterson). Grand Rapids, MI: Singspiration Music, Zondervan, Twentieth printing, 1974, #459.

Galli, Mark. "The Problem with Christus Victor," *Christianity Today*, April, 2011. https://www.christianitytoday.com/ct/2011/aprilweb-only/christusvicarious.html.

Good News Translation, Second Edition. New York, NY: American Bible Society, 1992.

Got Questions?org. https://www.gotquestions.org/.

Govier, Gordon. "Biblical Archeology's Top Ten Discoveries of 2018," *Christianity Today*, December 27, 2018. https://www.christianitytoday.com/news/2018/december/biblical-archaeology-top-10-discoveries-2018-israel.html.

Graham, Billy. "The Power of the Cross." *Decision Magazine*, April 2007. https://billygraham.org/decision-magazine/april-2007/the-power-of-the-cross/.

———. *The Reason for My Hope.* Nashville, TN: Thomas Nelson, 2013.

Graham, Franklin. *The Name.* Nashville, TN: Thomas Nelson, 2002.

Grounds, Vernon C. *YBH—Yes, But How?—Getting Serious About Your Faith.* Grand Rapids, MI: Discovery House, 1998.

Havergal, Frances Ridley. "Take My Life and Let It Be," 1874 (public domain). *Great Hymns of the Faith* (compiled and edited by John W. Peterson). Grand Rapids, MI: Singspiration Music, Zondervan, Twentieth printing, 1974, #393.

Bibliography

Havner, Vance. *Day by Day with Vance Havner—366 Devotions*. Grand Rapids, MI: Baker, 1984.

"Jacob Daniel DeShazer, 6584514, Staff Sergeant, Bombardier, Crew 16." Doolittle Tokyo Raiders. http://www.doolittleraider.com/raiders/deshazer.htm.

"Jewish Deicide." *Wikipedia*. https://en.wikipedia.org/wiki/Jewish_deicide.

Keene, Robert, Richard, or John. Or someone named Kirkham. Or John Keith. Authorship uncertain. "How Firm a Foundation," 1787 (public domain). *Great Hymns of the Faith* (compiled and edited by John W. Peterson). Grand Rapids, MI: Singspiration Music, Zondervan, Twentieth printing, 1974, #268.

Keener, Craig. *Gift & Giver: The Holy Spirit for Today*. Grand Rapids, MI: Baker Academic, 2001.

Kelly, Gerard. *Encounter with God*. Valley Forge, PA: Scripture Union, Oct/Nov/Dec 2010.

King Jr., Martin Luther. *A Testament of Hope: The Essential Writings and Speeches of Martin Luther King Jr.* New York City, NY: HarperOne, Reprint Edition, 2003.

———. *Stride toward Freedom: The Montgomery Story*. New York, NY: HarperCollins, 1958.

Lewis, C.S. *Mere Christianity*. New York, NY: Macmillan, 1943, 1945, 1952. Macmillan Paperbacks Edition, 1960. Eighth printing, 1967.

———. *The Problem of Pain*. New York, NY: HarperCollins, 1940/1996.

Lewis, Gordon, and Bruce Demarest. *Integrative Theology, Volume Two*. Grand Rapids, MI: Academie Books, Zondervan, 1990.

Lupton, Rosamund. *Sister*. New York City, NY: Crown/Archetype, Crown, Penguin Random House, 2011.

Luther, Martin. Sermon on Nov. 3, 1539 on John 1:29. *Daily Luther Quote*, #187. Milwaukee, WI: Northwestern Publishing. https://online.nph.net/.

MacDonald, William. *True Discipleship*. Oak Park, IL: Midwest Christian, 1962.

MacLeod, George F. *Only One Way Left*. Glasgow, Scotland: The Iona Community, 1956.

Mandryk, Jason. *Operation World*, Seventh Edition. Colorado Springs, CO: Biblica, 2010.

McDaniel, Debbie. "40 Powerful Quotes from Corrie ten Boom." Crosswalk.com, May 21, 2015. http://www.crosswalk.com/faith/spiritual-life/inspiring-quotes/40-powerful-quotes-from-corrie-ten-boom.html.

Mercer, Nick. *Encounter with God*. Valley Forge, PA: Scripture Union, Jan/Feb/Mar, 1999.

Metaxas, Eric. "Christian Hoarding?" *Breakpoint*, September 20, 2018.

———. "Real History, Toilets and All: Our Favorite Archeological Finds." *Breakpoint*, January 11, 2017.

———. "Transhumanists and the Quest for Godhead: Momento Mori." *Breakpoint*, February 28, 2017.

"Mother Teresa Quotes." http://www.quoteauthors.com/mother-teresa-quotes/.

Munger, Robert Boyd. *My Heart—Christ's Home*. Downers Grove, IL: InterVarsity, 1954.

Myers, Bill. "Dog Plucked to Safety After Mine Shaft Plunge." *The Denver Post*, December 8, 1970.

National World War II Museum, The. http://www.nationalww2museum.org/assets/pdfs/pearl-harbor-fact-sheet-1.pdf.

New International Version, The. Grand Rapids, MI: Zondervan, 1984.

Nicholson, James. "Whiter than Snow," 1872 (public domain). *Great Hymns of the Faith* (compiled and edited by John W. Peterson). Grand Rapids, MI: Singspiration Music, Zondervan, Twentieth printing, 1974, #310.

Bibliography

Oldfield, John. *Gut-Level Godliness: Authentic Shepherding in a Superficial Age.* Woodinville, WA: Augustus Ink, 2012.

Olson, Roger E. "Karl Barth's 'Jesus Loves Me, This I Know . . .' Answer: Can Anyone Verify It?" *Patheos: Hosting the Conversation on Faith,* Gordon-Conwell Theological Seminary, December 23, 2012. http://www.patheos.com/blogs/rogereolson/2012/12/karl-barths-jesus-loves-me-this-i-know-answer-can-anyone-verify-it/.

O'Reilly, Bill, and Martin Dugard. *Killing the Rising Sun: How America Vanquished World War II Japan.* New York, NY: Henry Holt, 2016.

Pacific War Online Encyclopedia, The. http://www.pwencycl.kgbudge.com/C/a/Casualties.htm.

Pascal, Blaise. *Pensees.* Paris, France: Port Royal, 1670.

Pershing, Ben. "Frank Wolf to Retire after 17 Terms in Congress." *The Washington Post,* December 17, 2013.

"Phil Cavarretta: The Hustling Cub Starred in Three World Series." *Baseball Almanac.* http://www.baseball-almanac.com/hero/hero2002b.shtml.

Piper, John. *What Jesus Demands from the World.* Wheaton, IL: Crossway, 2006.

Platt, David. *Radical: Taking Back Your Faith from the American Dream.* New York City, NY: Crown, 2010.

Premier International Fan Website for Mel Gibson's "The Passion of the Christ," The. http:// www.passion-movie.com/english/faq2.asp.

Ravenhill, Leonard. "Are We Willing to Drink His Cup?" (Sermon preached in 1985, quoted as Maxim #7). http://www.ravenhill.org/maxims7.htm. *Religion Today Summaries,* August 31, 2006.

Richardson, Bradford. "Human rights disaster: China's persecution of Christians at highest level since Mao." *The Washington Times,* June 6, 2018. https://www.washingtontimes.com/news/2018/jun/6/chinas-christian-persecution-highest-level-mao/.

Robinson, Robert. "Come, Thou Fount of Every Blessing," 1757 (public domain). *Great Hymns of the Faith* (compiled and edited by John W. Peterson). Grand Rapids, MI: Singspiration Music, Zondervan, Twentieth printing, 1974, #17.

Schaeffer, Francis. *How Should We Then Live? The Rise and Decline of Western Thought and Culture.* Old Tappan, NJ: Fleming H. Revell, 1976.

Shellnutt, Kate. "What It Was Like to Be Billy Graham's Pastor" (Interview with Don Wilton). *Christianity Today.* https://www.christianitytoday.com/ct/2018/february-web-only/billy-graham-pastor-don-wilton-funeral-interview.html?utm_source=ctweekly-html&utm_medium=Newsletter&utm_term=20177004&utm_content=567837372&utm_campaign=email.

Spurgeon, Charles. *Gleanings among the Sheaves.* New York, NY: Sheldon, 1869.

———. *The Complete Works of C. H. Spurgeon,* Volume 6, 1860, Sermons 286 to 347 (originally published in 1859 as the New Park Street Pulpit). Kindle Edition. Harrington, DE: Delmarva, 2013.

St. Augustine of Hippo Regius, Annaba, Algeria. Commentary on John 3:16–21. *Catholic Web Philosopher,* Wednesday, April 14, 2010. http://www.catholicwebphilosopher.com/2010/04/ god-so-loved-world-that-he-gave-his.html.

"Statistics on Americans and Body Piercing," April 20, 2014. http://www.tattooschool-art.com/blog/statistics-on-americans-and-body-piercing.

Stonestreet, John. "It Go Boom: Sodom, Pontius Pilate, and Archaeology." *Breakpoint,* December 21, 2018.

Tarr, Del. "God's Ways Are Unreasonable." *Leadership,* Spring Quarter, 1983.

Bibliography

"Tattoo Takeover: Three in Ten Americans Have Tattoos, and Most Don't Stop at Just One." February 10, 2016. http://www.theharrispoll.com/health-and-life/Tattoo_Takeover.html.

ten Boom, Corrie. "Corrie ten Boom on Forgiveness." *Guideposts*, November 1972.

Tenney, Merrill. *The Expositor's Bible Commentary with the New International Version of the Holy Bible*, Volume 9. Grand Rapids, MI: Zondervan, 1981.

Thoreau, Henry David. *Walden*. Boston: Ticknor and Fields, 1854.

Toplady, Augustus. "Rock of Ages," 1763 (public domain). *Great Hymns of the Faith* (compiled and edited by John W. Peterson). Grand Rapids, MI: Singspiration Music, Zondervan, Twentieth printing, 1974, #126.

Turner, Jennifer. "Confess and Be Restored." *Encounter with God*. Valley Forge, PA: Scripture Union, Jan/Feb/Mar 2017.

Ultimate List of Online Giving Statistics for 2017, The. https://nonprofitssource.com/online-giving-statistics/.

Vitale, Vince. "If God, Why Suffering?" Ravi Zacharias International Ministries, August 28, 2014. http://rzim.org/just-thinking/if-god-why-suffering/.

Watts, Isaac. "Alas! And Did My Savior Bleed?" 1707 (public domain). *Great Hymns of the Faith* (compiled and edited by John W. Peterson). Grand Rapids, MI: Singspiration Music, Zondervan, Twentieth printing, 1974, #110.

———. "Am I a Soldier of the Cross?" 1724 (public domain). *Great Hymns of the Faith* (compiled and edited by John W. Peterson). Grand Rapids, MI: Singspiration Music, Zondervan, Twentieth printing, 1974, #414.

———. "When I Survey the Wondrous Cross," 1707 (public domain). *Great Hymns of the Faith* (compiled and edited by John W. Peterson). Grand Rapids, MI: Singspiration Music, Zondervan, Twentieth printing, 1974, #118.

Wesley, Charles. "O for a Thousand Tongues to Sing," 1739 (public domain). *Great Hymns of the Faith* (compiled and edited by John W. Peterson). Grand Rapids, MI: Singspiration Music, Zondervan, Twentieth printing, 1974, #46.

Wesley, John. *A Plain Account of Christian Perfection* (1767). Kansas City, MO: Beacon Hill, 1966.

———. *The Works of the Rev. John Wesley: Forty-two sermons on various subjects*. New York, NY: J. & J. Harper, 1826.

Woodward, Kenneth. "A Lesser Child of God." *Newsweek*, April 4, 1994.

Yancey, Philip. *Where Is God When It Hurts?* Grand Rapids, MI: Zondervan, 1977.

Young, Robert. *Young's Literal Translation of the Holy Bible* (originally published in 1862). Ada, MI: Baker, 1989.

Zacharias, Ravi. *Cries of the Heart*. Nashville, TN: Thomas Nelson, 2002.

Zhand, Brian. "How Does 'Dying for Our Sins' Work?" April 16, 2014. http://brianzahnd.com/2014/04/dying-sins-work/.

Zondervan NASB (New American Standard Bible) Study Bible, The. Grand Rapids, MI: Zondervan, 1999.

www.ingramcontent.com/pod-product-compliance
Lightning Source LLC
Chambersburg PA
CBHW062038220426
43662CB00010B/1553